Life Events as Stressors in Childhood and Adolescence

DEVELOPMENTAL CLINICAL PSYCHOLOGY AND PSYCHIATRY SERIES

Series Editor: **Alan E. Kazdin**

In the Series:

Forthcoming:

Life Events as Stressors in Childhood and Adolescence

James H. Johnson

Volume 8.
Developmental Clinical Psychology and Psychiatry

SAGE PUBLICATIONS
The Publishers of Professional Social Science
Newbury Park   Beverly Hills   London   New Delhi

Copyright © 1986 by Sage Publications, Inc.

For information address:

SAGE Publications, Inc.
275 South Beverly Drive
Beverly Hills, California 90212

SAGE Publications Inc.
2111 West Hillcrest Drive
Newbury Park
California 91320

SAGE Publications Ltd.
28 Banner Street
London EC1Y 8QE
England

SAGE PUBLICATIONS India Pvt. Ltd.
M-32 Market
Greater Kailash I
New Delhi 110 048 India

Printed in the United States of America

Library of Congress Cataloging-in-Publication Data

Main entry under title:

Johnson, James H. (James Harmon), 1943-
  Life events as stressors in childhood and adolescence.

  (Developmental clinical psychology and psychiatry
series ; v. 8)
  Bibliography: p.
  Includes index.
  1. Stress in children.   2. Life change events—Psy-
chological aspects.   3. Adolescent psychology.
I. Title.   II. Series: Developmental clinical psychology
and psychiatry ; v. 8.
BF723.S75J64   1986   155.4   86-1948
ISBN 0-8039-2725-8
ISBN 0-8039-2726-6 (pbk.)

FIRST PRINTING

CONTENTS

To Theda, Jamie, and Trey
and Jamie's friends
Jonathan, Judy, and Bretts

SERIES EDITOR'S INTRODUCTION

Interest in child development and adjustment is by no means new. Yet only recently has the study of children benefited from advances in both clinical and scientific research. Many reasons might explain the recent systematic attention to children, including more pervasive advances in research in the social and biological sciences, the emergence of disciplines and subdisciplines that focus exclusively on childhood and adolescence, and greater appreciation of the impact of such influences as family, peers, school, and many other factors on child adjustment. Apart from interest in the study of child development and adjustment for its own sake, the need to address clinical problems of adulthood naturally draws one to investigation of precursors in childhood and adolescence.

Within a relatively brief period, the study of psychopathology and mental health among children and adolescents has evolved and proliferated considerably. In fact, several different professional journals, annual book series, and handbooks devoted entirely to the study of children and adolescents and their adjustment document the proliferation of work in the field. Although many different disciplines and specialty areas contribute to knowledge of disorders that emerge in the course of development, there is a paucity of resource material that presents information in an authoritative, systematic, and disseminable fashion. There is a need within the field to convey the latest developments and to represent different disciplines, multiple approaches to, and conceptual views of the topics of childhood and adolescent adjustment and maladjustment.

The Sage series, Developmental Clinical Psychology and Psychiatry, is designed to serve uniquely several needs of the field. The series encompasses individual monographs prepared by experts in the fields of clinical child psychology, child psychiatry, child development, and related disciplines. The primary focus is on childhood psychopathology, which refers broadly here to the diagnosis, assessment, treatment, and prevention of problems that arise in the period of infancy through adolescence. A working assumption of the series is that understanding, identifying, and treating problems of youth cannot be resolved by narrow, single discipline, and parochial conceptual views. Thus the series is necessarily broad and draws upon multiple disciplines and diverse views within a given discipline.

The task for individual contributors is to present the latest theory and research on various topics, including specific types of dysfunction, diagnostic and treatment approaches, and special problem areas that affect adjustment. Core topics within clinical work are addressed by the series. Authors are asked to bridge potential theory, research, and clinical practice, and to outline the current status and future directions. The goals of the series and the tasks presented to individual contributors are demanding. We have been extremely fortunate in recruiting leaders in the fields who have been able to translate their recognized scholarship and expertise into highly readable works on contemporary topics.

The present book considers the topic of life events as stressors in childhood and adolescence. Life events and stressors have been actively studied in recent years in part because of the recognition of their role in diverse psychological disorders, health and health-related problems, and adjustment in general. Research with children and adolescents has followed on the heels of parallel work with adults. Yet the area has clearly developed its own body of findings, measures, and theoretical work. Dr. James H. Johnson, author of the present monograph, is in a unique position in the field. He has investigated life events with children, adolescents, and adults. Moreover, he has contributed significantly to the assessment of life events and to our understanding of the variables that influence their impact. The book provides a concise integration of the latest findings on the impact of life events on health and adjustment, the extent and limits of current knowledge, and the major questions that face the field. The book is of special relevance to the series because of the pervasive influence of stressful events for children, adolescents, and their families.

—Alan E. Kazdin, Ph.D.
Series Editor

PREFACE

Research dealing with the effects of stressful life changes on the health and adjustment of adults has proliferated rapidly within the past 15 to 20 years. By now there are well over a thousand papers dealing with adult life stress as well as numerous books and book chapters devoted specifically to this topic.

As is frequently the case with work in other areas, research dealing with life stress in childhood and adolescence has lagged behind that with adults. But things are changing. Within the last several years the number of publications related to child/adolescent life stress has increased significantly. A quick count of papers and book chapters in this area turned up a total of 38 appearing during the past five years. This can be contrasted with a total of 10 appearing during the previous five-year period. Although the reliability of this count has not been confirmed and there may have been a paper here or there that was missed, these figures do seem to suggest a rapidly developing interest in the effects of life events on younger age groups.

Research in this area has resulted in the development of new assessment measures and attention being given to factors that may make children and adolescents more or less vulnerable to the effects of stress, as well as additional information concerning the correlates of cumulative life change. This work has also provided us with information regarding the types of life events that are most highly correlated with child and adolescent problems as well as some information concerning those that may be related to more positive outcomes. Despite these recent advances, child/adolescent life stress research is still in its infancy; a review of the literature suggests that there are currently more questions than answers regarding the precise link between life changes and outcomes. More work in this area is clearly needed. This book reviews what has been accomplished to date, considers conceptual and methodological issues relevant to interpreting the results of research studies, and addresses several priorities for future research.

Given that children and adolescents experience a range of disruptive life changes during the process of development (e.g., changes in residence, changing schools, parental separation, divorce, death of a parent) and that cumulative changes of this type often appear to be associated with negative outcomes, it seems imperative that we continue to explore the conditions under which these sorts of potential stressors lead to negative outcomes, and the ways we can best help children and adolescents learn to cope with them. It is hoped that this book will encourage others to add to our knowledge in this area.

Books are always influenced by colleagues, students, and others that one has worked with and been influenced by. This one is no exception. In this regard a special acknowledgment is due Irwin Sarason, who first introduced me to the area of life stress research. As a research collaborator, valued colleague, and friend, he is not only responsible for my involvement in this area but has also greatly influenced my thinking regarding issues related to life stress. The influence of Judy Siegel, an early assistant and collaborator in our life stress research who is now a productive researcher in her own right, should also be acknowledged.

Finally, I would like to express a special note of gratitude to my wife, Theda, and my children, Jamie and Trey, for understanding why I spent more time at the office than at home while preoccupied with the completion of this manuscript. This book is dedicated to them.

1

LIFE EVENTS AND THEIR RELATIONSHIP TO HEALTH AND ADJUSTMENT
An Introduction

Jason, a 10-year-old, was referred for psychological evaluation by his pediatrician, who indicated that Jason's behavior and general level of functioning were increasingly becoming a source of concern to his father, who had asked that the referral be made. During the intake evaluation Jason's father indicated that although his son had never excelled in school, his grades during the past year had dropped significantly and that he had received all failing grades during the most recent grading period. He noted that Jason's behavior had become progressively more difficult to manage in the past two or three months and that on several occasions Jason had "really gotten out of control" when being reprimanded and had attempted to run away. On other occasions Jason was said to have become extremely angry without any major provocation and to have torn up several of his toys as well as some that belonged to his younger sister. The father also reported that Jason had recently seemed quite depressed and that on one occasion, after watching a TV show dealing with childhood suicide, indicated that he understood how the children depicted in the program felt. This incident greatly troubled the father and served as the major impetus for the referral.

In obtaining a family history it was learned that the parents were divorced when Jason was approximately 2½ years of age. As the mother reportedly indicated little interest in the children, the father was given legal custody of both Jason and his sister. Approximately six months after the divorce Jason's younger sister was diagnosed as having a chronic and life-threatening kidney disorder that would ultimately require transplantation. At the time of the interview the father indicated that his daughter had since been in and out of the hospital on many occasions and that although her condition was now reasonably stable, it could worsen rapidly at any time. Regarding other significant life history events, the father stated that within a couple years of the divorce his ex-wife appeared to have a "change of heart" regarding custody of the children and on two occasions kidnapped Jason and his sister. On one of these occasions the children were returned to the father after only a short period of time. On the other occasion they were taken out of state and returned only after what was described as a rather bitter custody fight. Since that time the children had not seen the mother because of a court order that prohibited her from having contact with them. The father noted that he and the children had lived in several different locations during the past five or six years and that his ex-wife currently did not know where they were living.

The father indicated that he remarried approximately three and a half years ago and that both of the children had been very unhappy about the marriage. The marriage ended in divorce after only eight months. Reasons given by the father for the divorce were that his wife did not care for children or enjoy being a mother. Only after the marriage did he learn that his wife previously had a child whom she had voluntarily given up for adoption.

Commenting that the family had been through a lot, the father emphasized that the past six months or so had been especially difficult for Jason. Here he noted that approximately six months ago, while Jason was watching his favorite uncle trying to train a horse, the uncle fell off and the horse fell on top of him. This resulted in a severe head injury, the need for an immediate tracheotomy, and Jason's uncle being permanently blinded in both eyes. As Jason was with the uncle at the time of the accident, it was an exceptionally traumatic event for him and one that continues to bother him, according to the father. To compound the family's problems further, while in the hospital the uncle developed a relationship with the nurse who was caring for him, and they were married within a month of his release from the hospital. The father stated that Jason was very happy about the marriage and quickly became friends with his uncle's wife, who treated him as if he were "special." Two months after the marriage, without apparent warning, she committed suicide.

Although it is commonplace for adults to think of childhood as a time free of the pressures and troubles that confront them and perhaps, under times of stress, to wish they could reexperience what they recall as the more carefree days of their youth, cases like Jason's emphasize that for some, childhood is a period marked by extreme stress. Indeed, there is an increasing belief on the part of psychologists, psychiatrists, and pediatricians that stress experienced by children and adolescents may play an important role in the development of various types of health and adjustment problems.

Children are exposed in varying degrees and in different ways to a wide range of situations that require coping and adaptation. Most experience the arrival of new brothers or sisters, the accompanying changes in family routines, and the frequent feelings of jealousy that result from having to share parental attention with a new family member. All must deal with separation issues associated with entering school for the first time. Many change from one school to another, move to a new home or perhaps a new community, and are faced with leaving behind old friendships, attempting to develop new ones, and adjusting to new and unfamiliar surroundings. Many children are exposed to the stress resulting from conflict between their parents, and increasing numbers of children are forced to cope with all the feelings and life changes that come with parental separation or divorce. A smaller but still significant number experience the serious illness or death of a parent or other family member. And some are themselves faced with serious illnesses or major physical disabilities and the stress of repeated hospitalizations and intrusive medical procedures that these conditions sometimes require. This is to say nothing of those seemingly trivial (to adults) but more frequently occurring stressors that some children experience, such as being made fun of by others, not being asked to a birthday party, being the last person selected for the team at recess—all of which may be experienced as stressful when they occur.

It is clear that for many childhood is far from being the trouble-free time we sometimes reminisce about when burdened by the demands of adult life. For some it is a time marked by extremely stressful events and life transitions that would severely tax the coping and adaptational abilities of even the most resilient child.

The developing awareness of stress as a potential contributor to the problems of childhood has resulted in increased attention being given to the effects of stressful life changes on children and adolescents. This book is about these "real-life" stressors of childhood and represents an attempt to convey what is currently known (and what we need to learn) about the effects of stressful life changes on children and youth. The chapters that follow will focus on methods of assessing life changes experienced by children and adolescents, the impact of major life changes on the state of the child's physical health and psychological adjustment, and individual differences in children's response to stress that render certain children more or less vulnerable. Possible ways of helping children and adolescents deal with the stressors they experience will also be considered. Before addressing these topics, however, it is important to provide some background in order to place the discussion of child life stress in perspective.

THE CONCEPT OF STRESS

Any discussion of stress requires that at least some attention be given to how the concept is to be used. Despite the fact that the word "stress" is a part of almost everyone's vocabulary and that most of us have some subjective notion of what it means to be "stressed" (e.g., we are under pressure, we are tense, we are anxious, we feel overwhelmed, we experience more troublesome situations than we can deal with), those working in the area have used the concept in a variety of ways and frequently disagree as to how the term should be defined. A brief discussion of what are perhaps the three most popular ways of viewing stress is presented in the sections that follow.

Stimulus-Oriented Views

For many, stress is defined as the experiencing of specific types of stimuli. From this stimulus-oriented perspective, stress is seen as resulting from experiencing any of a number of situations that are noxious or threatening or that place excessive demands on the individual. For example, the undergraduate research subject who is told that he or she may be given an electric shock while performing an experimental task would be presumed to be performing under stress. So would the subject who is required to perform while immersing his or her arm in a bucket of ice water for an extended period of time or who is required to listen to bursts of noise through earphones while participating in an experiment. In a more real-life context, experiencing natural disasters such as floods, hurricanes, earthquakes, or conditions of war are assumed to result in stress. Likewise, persons experiencing major life events (e.g., divorce, death in the family, changes in residence, loss of job) or a large number of daily hassles (e.g., dealing with inconsiderate people, having to pick up the slack for a lazy coworker) are often assumed to be under stress (Lazarus & Folkman, 1985). There are still other less obvious (in the sense of being more private) stimuli that would also be seen as stressful. Examples of these sorts of stressors might be the knowledge that one has previously been exposed to what is known to be a potent carcinogen, one's knowledge of a strong family history of heart disease, and so forth.

From this perspective, then, stress is defined in terms of forces—either within the person or within the environment—that affect the individual. Basic to this view is the belief that there are many identifiable stimuli or situations that invariably result in stress if experienced; the more of these situations experienced, the higher the level of stress. As will be seen later, these views are reflected in much of the life stress literature where it has been assumed that *all* major life changes are stressful because of the social readjustment they require, and that stress can be indexed in terms of the number of life events experienced within a given period of time.

Although I will have more to say about this later, it may be noted that this position fails to consider adequately the possibility that individuals may view "potential stressors" differently and that what may be stressful for one person may not be stressful for another. To the extent that there are individual differences in responding to potentially stressful aspects of one's environment, defining stress in this manner has significant limitations.

Response-Oriented Views

Rather than focusing on the degree of exposure to stressful stimuli (and assuming that stress can be indexed in this manner), others working in the area have focused on the organism's biological or psychological response to presumably stressful situations. This response-oriented perspective is perhaps most clearly reflected in the views of noted stress researcher Hans Selye, whose pioneering work has served as a stimulus for much of the present-day work related to stress and its effects on the individual.

Based on his early work with animals exposed to a range of noxious stimuli, Selye (1936) attempted to characterize the organism's response to continued stress in terms of what has been called the General Adaptation Syndrome (GAS). According to this model, the initial response to any stressor is an *alarm reaction* that involves a generalized mobilization of the body's defensive forces, which are designed to enable the organism to cope with the situation. During this stage the organism may experience a range of physiological changes in preparation for dealing with the situation. Included here are alterations in heart rate, respiration, and skin resistance, along with changes in biochemical indices of sympathetic nervous system activation (e.g., the secretion of increased levels of epinephrine and norepinephrine and subsequent increases in blood sugar levels). Selye also demonstrated a number of structural changes that are associated with the alarm stage, including adrenal cortical enlargement, atrophy of the thymus and other lymphatic structures, and the development of bleeding ulcers of the stomach and duodenum.

With the continuation of stress this alarm reaction is followed by a *stage of resistance*. In this second stage, many of the bodily processes activated during the alarm phase return to somewhat more normal levels. However, despite the fact that the organism appears to "adapt" to the continued stress and may seem to be coping, the resistance of the organism is reduced and the ability to deal with new or increased levels of stress is significantly diminished. This continued exposure to stress gradually depletes what Selye (1982) has referred to as *adaptational energy,* or the body's resources and ability to deal with new demands made on it.

Although the final stage of the General Adaptation Syndrome is usually not reached, if the organism experiences continued stress for an extended period of time or if the situation is significantly compounded by experiencing new stressors, a stage of *exhaustion* may be reached. In this stage, the organism's coping abilities become inadequate to deal with the situation and the final result may be death. It should be noted again that psychological stressors seldom result in the person reaching this final stage; this typically occurs only when he or she is faced with extremely adverse physical conditions, such as prolonged exposure to heat or cold (Selye, 1982).

In his research on the GAS, Selye found that many of the physiological changes associated with the alarm reaction (e.g., adrenal cortical enlargement, atrophy of lymphatic structures, development of stomach and duodenal ulcers) occurred in response to a broad range of stressful stimuli. These included such diverse stimuli as cold, heat, and nervous irritation as well as stimuli capable of increasing psychological arousal (Selye, 1982). These findings led him to conclude that such biological changes represented the response of the body to *any* stressor, that these changes represent objective indicators of stress, and that stress can best be defined as a general nonspecific bodily response to any demand made upon it. Rather than assessing stress by considering the degree of exposure to noxious or threatening stimuli, this perspective argues that stress should be assessed by considering the organism's response to presumably stressful aspects of the environment.

Although important issues have been raised regarding the adequacy of this point of view (Mason, 1975), researchers often define stress in terms of the individual's responses to various aspects of the environment. Thus stress is often inferred because the person is tense, anxious, depressed (indeed, stress is often treated as synonymous with these constructs), because he or she displays physical signs of arousal or activation, or because the individual shows certain biochemical changes (e.g., secretion of corticosteroids and catecholamines) that are often associated with the experiencing of adverse environmental circumstances (Baum, Grunberg, & Singer, 1982).

Despite the fact that researchers defining stress in this way have often made important contributions to the literature, such response-oriented views have certain limitations. For example, the failure of an individual to display what are assumed to be signs of stress when confronted with a presumably stressful stimulus may suggest either that the stimulus was not really stressful or that the responses being assessed are not invariant indicators of stress, even though the stimulus may have actually been "stressful" to the person. An additional limitation is the inability to specify which stimuli are stressful independent of the person's response to them. Clearly the degree of ambiguity inherent in such an approach is likely to stand in the way of advances in our knowledge regarding the relationship between stressful stimuli and their impact on the individual.

Stress as a Transaction
Between Person and Environment

In response to the limitations of stimulus-oriented and response-oriented views, some stress researchers choose to define stress in terms of transactions between the person and the environment. From this perspective it might be argued that the stressfulness of environmental events is heavily dependent on the person's view of these events (e.g., whether they see them as threatening or nonthreatening, desirable or undesirable, controllable or uncontrollable, and so forth), and that the impact of potential stressors on the individual depends on the available resources the individual has for dealing with these events. Thus it is assumed that what is stressful for one person may not be stressful for another, and given the same level of stress, some persons may be affected to a greater or lesser degree than others. From this viewpoint it is inappropriate to define stress simply in terms of the number of presumed stressors experienced (as these may or may not be stressful for a given individual). Likewise, it would be inappropriate to define stress in terms of the individual's response to "stressors" as, even in the face of stress, all individuals may not show the same adverse reactions.

Although this more cognitively oriented view has been embraced by many who work in this area, it is best reflected in the writings of Lazarus and his colleagues (see Lazarus, 1966; Lazarus & Folkman, 1985; Lazarus & Launier, 1978). In terms of a specific definition, Lazarus and Folkman (1985, p. 19) offer the following: "Psychological stress is a particular relationship between the person and the environment that is appraised by the person as taxing or exceeding his or her resources and endangering his or her well-being." This definition is consistent with the views outlined above in terms of placing an emphasis on transactions between the person and the environment and on those cognitive variables and mediational processes that are central to the experiencing of stress. From this point of view, stress results from experiencing events or situations that are *seen by individuals* as threatening or as placing demands on them that exceed their ability to cope. Central to this view is the concept of appraisal.

At a very general level, cognitive appraisal is the process through which a person evaluates any encounter with a potential stressor in terms of its significance for well-being (Lazarus & Folkman, 1985). Two basic types of appraisal are relevant.

Primary Appraisal. This type of appraisal has to do with the person's view of a given situation in terms of its threat value and can be one of three types. The stimulus or situation can be appraised as *irrelevant*; it is seen as having no implications, either positive or negative, for the person. It can be appraised as *benign-positive,* likely to lead to some desirable outcome. Or a situation can be appraised as *stressful.* Stress appraisals can, in turn, take several forms. An event might be appraised as having already resulted in significant harm or loss, as in the case of a serious illness or injury or the loss of a significant other (harm/loss appraisal). An event might be appraised as being likely to have a negative impact, in the form of harm or loss, at some time in the future (threat appraisal). Finally, a situation may be appraised as a challenge. Although challenge appraisals differ from threat appraisals because they focus on the "potential for gain or growth inherent in an encounter" with the environment (Lazarus & Folkman, 1985, p. 33), they are seen as stressful in that they require the mobilization of coping resources and involve the risk of failure—a fact which suggests that appraisals of threat and challenge are not mutually exclusive or unrelated. This process of primary appraisal involves making a range of complex and interrelated judgments regarding the nature of situations and their implication for the person.

Secondary Appraisal. Whereas primary appraisals have to do with the relevance of environmental events vis-à-vis the person's well-being, secondary appraisals concern the individual's appraisal of the resources available for dealing with threatening or challenging situations. As Lazarus and Folkman (1985) have suggested, primary appraisal has to do with what is at stake, and secondary appraisal has more to do with what can be accomplished. As these authors have indicated, this sort of appraisal is more than simply thinking through the things that might be done. In their words, it involves "a complex evaluative process that takes into account which coping options are available, the likelihood that a given coping option will accomplish what it is supposed to, and the likelihood that one can apply a particular strategy or set of strategies effectively" (p. 35).

In considering these notions of primary and secondary appraisal, it should be pointed out that appraisals of events and situations are not simply a one-shot affair. Indeed, individuals often engage in reappraisals of situations based on new information that might be obtained. Such reappraisals may lead to a different view of the stressfulness of the situation or to different approaches to coping.

This short discussion is inadequate to describe fully either the theory or the research related to Lazarus's views of stress and emotion; however, it should sufficiently illustrate this alternate way of viewing stress-related phenomena. From this perspective, the degree of stress experienced by an individual is determined not only by those potential stressors to which he or she is exposed but also by the person's appraisals of these potential stressors. The general notion of appraisals (and other mediating variables) and their relevance for understanding the potential effects of life changes on children and adolescents will be considered in the chapters to follow.

Definitions of Stress: An Overview

When one considers that stress is sometimes defined as experiencing "stressors," sometimes defined on the basis of a person's responses to stimuli that are presumed to be stressors, and sometimes on the basis of an interaction of the person and environment, it is obvious why some have questioned the heuristic value of the concept. Many investigators shy away from research in this area; others use the term "stress" with apparent misgivings, if at all (Garmezy, 1983). Nevertheless, the concept of stress has proven to be an extremely enduring one that continues to have strong appeal to layperson and professional alike (Rutter, 1983).

The appeal of this concept probably relates to the fact that both children and adults do experience aversive, psychologically threatening, or otherwise troublesome situations and that these experiences sometimes correlate with negative outcomes. In such instances the term "stress" represents a convenient way of attempting to characterize what is *assumed* to be going on within the organism and intervening between stimulus and response. Viewed in this way, "stress" can be thought of simply as a useful construct denoting a hypothetical state of the organism that is linked to various types of environmental stimuli (as these are perceived by the individual) on one hand and to various outcomes on the other.

Even without adopting a specific definition of stress (although the way the term will be used here is generally consistent with the views of

Lazarus and his colleagues—see Lazarus & Folkman, 1985), it is quite appropriate to speak of potential stressors and their impact on the individual (as this impact is reflected in cognitive, behavioral, and/or physiological changes) and the degree to which the relationship between potential stressors and various outcomes are mediated by other variables. Taking this approach, this book focuses on the relationship between life changes experienced by children and adolescents and the extent to which these changes are related to problems of health and adjustment.

CORRELATES OF STRESSFUL LIFE EVENTS: AN OVERVIEW OF THE ADULT LITERATURE

Although this book is about life changes experienced by children and adolescents, much of the work in this area has focused on adults. There is now, in fact, a sizable body of literature dealing with the assessment of life changes in adults, the correlates of stressful life events in adults, and variables that appear to moderate the impact of stressful life changes in older individuals. Because research with children and adolescents has lagged behind that with adults and to some extent has been modeled after it, a brief review of this work is necessary in order to place the findings with children and adolescents in perspective. For those interested in more detailed coverage of the adult literature, the following are suggested: Dohrenwend and Dohrenwend (1981), Monroe (1982), Sarason, Sarason, and Johnson (1985), and Thoits (1983).

Assessing Life Changes

Psychologists, psychiatrists, and others have for many years commented on a relationship between stressful life changes and problems of health and adjustment, but systematic research into the correlates of life stress is a relatively recent phenomenon. Indeed, much of the work in this area can be traced to the publication by Holmes and Rahe, in 1967, of an article describing an attempt to quantify the impact of cumulative life changes. This work culminated in the development of an assessment instrument, the Schedule of Recent Experiences (SRE), which has been widely used in subsequent research. The widespread use of this measure is no doubt related to the fact that it provided the first convenient index not only of the extent of life changes experienced but also of their cumulative impact. The important role of the SRE as a stimulus to research in this area merits a brief description.

The SRE consists of a listing of the 43 events listed in Table 1.1. Persons respond to these events by indicating, for each item, whether they have experienced that event during the recent past and, if so, the number of times the event was experienced. Life stress scores are arrived at by summing values, termed *life change units,* associated with those events that have been experienced. To obtain these life change units Holmes and Rahe had large numbers of subjects rate each of the 43 events with regard to the amount of adjustment they required. Specifically, the item "marriage" was assigned an arbitrary value of 500 and was used as a standard anchor point in rating the other events. Subjects were asked to rate the other events by assigning values above or below 500 to reflect the degree to which these events required, on the average, more or less social readjustment than marriage. Average readjustment ratings were then obtained for each event. These values, or *life change units*, when divided by the constant 10, were assumed to represent an index of the stressfulness of each of the events included in the measure. To illustrate, marriage is given a value of 50, death of a spouse the value of 100, pregnancy a value of 40, changes in financial status a value of 38, and minor violations of the law a value of 11. As noted above, a total life stress score is obtained by determining those events experienced by the person and summing the life change units associated with these events. This total score is purported to reflect the degree of life stress experienced by the person within a specified time interval, usually one or two years. (For a more detailed overview of the development and the psychometric properties of the SRE, see Holmes & Masuda, 1974.)

Although the adequacy of the SRE as a measure of life stress has been questioned on a number of counts (Johnson & Sarason, 1979a; Monroe, 1982; Sarason, Johnson, & Siegel, 1978; Sarason, Sarason, & Johnson, 1985; Thoits, 1983) and alternative measures have been proposed to assess both major life changes (see Dohrenwend, Krasnoff, Askenasy, & Dohrenwend, 1978; Sarason, Johnson, & Siegel,

TABLE 1.1
SRE Life Events and Associated Life Change Units

Rank	Life Event	Mean Value
1	Death of spouse	100
2	Divorce	73
3	Marital separation	65
4	Jail term	63
5	Death of close family member	63
6	Personal injury or illness	53
7	Marriage	50
8	Fired at work	47
9	Marital reconciliation	45
10	Retirement	45
11	Change in health of family member	44
12	Pregnancy	40
13	Sex difficulties	39
14	Gain of new family member	39
15	Business readjustment	39
16	Change in financial state	38
17	Death of close friend	37
18	Change to different line of work	36
19	Change in number of arguments with spouse	35
20	Mortgage over $10,000	31
21	Foreclosure of mortgage or loan	30
22	Change in responsibilities at work	29
23	Son or daughter leaving home	29
24	Trouble with in-laws	29
25	Outstanding personal achievement	28
26	Wife begin or stop work	26
27	Begin or end school	26
28	Change in living conditions	25
29	Revision of personal habits	24
30	Trouble with boss	23
31	Change in work hours or conditions	20
32	Change in residence	20
33	Change in schools	20
34	Change in recreation	19
35	Change in church activities	19
36	Change in social activities	18
37	Mortgage or loan less than $10,000	17
38	Change in sleeping habits	16
39	Change in number of family get-togethers	15
40	Change in eating habits	15
41	Vacation	13
42	Christmas	12
43	Minor violations of the law	11

SOURCE: Holmes and Rahe (1967). Reprinted with permission.

1978) and daily stressors (Kanner, Coyne, Schaefer, & Lazarus, 1981), the SRE, or variations on this measure, have been employed in most of the more than 1,000 life stress studies published to date (Holmes, 1979). This measure has also served as the prototype for the development of the most popular approach to child life stress assessment, to be described in Chapter 2.

Life Stress and Physical Illness

Many adult life stress studies have been concerned with the relationship between life change and physical health problems. Although it is possible to find fault with many of these investigations on both methodological and conceptual grounds, taken together they appear to provide general support for a relationship between life stress and a range of physical health outcomes.

Several group studies have found a relationship between increased levels of life stress and illness rates (Rahe, Mahan, & Arthur, 1970; Rubin, Gunderson, & Arthur, 1971) and the utilization of health services (Gortmaker, Eckenrode, & Gore, 1982). Studies have found significant relationships between life stress and specific types of physical health outcomes, such as cardiac death and myocardial infarction (Edwards, 1971; Lundberg, Theorell & Lind, 1975; Rahe & Lind, 1971; Rahe & Paaskivi, 1971; Theorell & Rahe, 1971), hypertension (Lal, Ahuja, & Madhukar, 1982), pregnancy and birth complications (Gorsuch & Key, 1974; Nuckolls, Cassell, & Kaplan, 1972), and menstrual discomfort (Siegel, Johnson, & Sarason, 1979). Life stress has been found to relate to symptom severity, degree of control over illness, and recurrent symptoms in individuals displaying various chronic illnesses such as asthma (de Araujo, Van Arsdel, Holmes, & Dudley, 1973), diabetes (Bradley, 1979), and genital herpes (Watson, 1983). Still other studies have found relationships between life stress and both athletic injuries (Bramwell, Wagner, Masuda, & Holmes, 1975) and work-related accidents (Levenson, Hirschfeld, Hirschfeld, & Dzubay, 1983). Finally, Wyler, Masuda, and Holmes (1971) also found a significant relationship between extent of experienced life stress and seriousness of illness, higher levels of life stress being correlated with more serious types of illness.

The studies cited here represent only a sampling of those suggesting a relationship between life changes and health-related variables; still, it should be obvious that at least among adults, life stress is correlated with a diverse array of physical health problems. These findings are consistent with the views of life stress researchers such as Holmes and Masuda (1974), who have suggested that stressful life changes contribute to the development of a range of physical problems by increasing susceptibility to illness. Given exposure to some pathogenic agent or a predisposition to develop a given disorder, life stress is seen as increasing the likelihood of illness and/or as having an influence on the timing of disease onset through lowering the individual's resistance. Thus life stress is seen as contributing to health problems not directly but through its interaction with other biological or environmental factors. Despite the plausible nature of this hypothesis, we actually know little regarding the mechanism(s) through which life stress may increase the likelihood of health-related problems, although a number of recent studies suggest that experiencing certain stressors can influence immunocompetence, thus perhaps making the person more susceptible to a range of health risks (Jermott & Locke, 1984).

Life Stress and Psychological Adjustment

Other studies have focused on the relationship between life changes and indices of psychological adjustment. Significant correlates of life stress are found here as well. Several studies, for example, have documented a relationship between life stress and measures of anxiety (Dekker & Webb, 1974; Lauer, 1973), psychological distress (Dohrenwend, 1973), and reports of psychiatric symptoms (Myers, Lindenthal, & Pepper, 1974). Paykel (1974) likewise reported a relationship between cumulative life changes and clinical depression, as well as suicide attempts. And Monroe, Bellack, Hersen, and Himmelhoch (1983) found a relationship between the experiencing of life changes and the course of depressive disorder. Other studies have found patients with various types of psychiatric disorders to be distinguishable from nonpsychiatric controls in terms of the level of life changes experienced (Dekker & Webb, 1974; Paykel, 1974). Additional investigations have also found support for relationships between life changes and child abuse (Egeland, Breitenbucher, & Rosenberg, 1981;

Gaines, Sandgrund, Green, & Power, 1978; Justice & Duncan, 1976), as well as lowered academic (Carranza, 1972) and work (Harris, 1972) performance. As in the case of physical health correlates, the studies cited here represent only a small sample of those suggesting a relationship between life changes and adjustment-related variables.

Commentary

Having cited a number of studies supporting a link between stressful life changes and problems of health and adjustment, it is necessary to add a note of caution. Many of these studies have used measures of life change that can be faulted on both methodological and conceptual grounds. Many have employed indices of health and adjustment that represent less than adequate dependent measures. Many have relied on a retrospective recall of life changes that may have biased findings to some unknown degree. And all of the studies have been of a correlational nature, making it impossible to make inferences regarding causality (although a causal relationship in which life events contribute to health and adjustment problems is usually assumed).

Other problems of interpretation arise from the fact that life change measures themselves often include events that could be viewed as manifestations or the consequences of health or adjustment problems (e.g., being fired from one's job; having sexual difficulties). To the extent that the occurrence of such events reflects problems of health or adjustment, their inclusion may result in spurious correlations due to the confounding of independent and dependent measures. In addition to having to take into account these methodological issues (all of which will be considered in greater detail with reference to the child literature), most studies have simply dealt with assessing direct linear relationships between life changes and stress-related variables, rather than considering that individuals may differ in the extent to which they are affected by life changes. Recent studies documenting the role of social (e.g., social support) and individual difference variables (e.g., locus of control, stimulation seeking) as moderators of life stress suggest that studies that fail to consider the possibility that life stress may have different effects on different individuals may be seriously limited.

These problems notwithstanding, the adult literature as a whole provides reasonable support for a general relationship between cumulative life changes and problems of physical health and psychological adjustment. However, the nature of this relationship is not a simple or direct one, and the actual impact of life change on the individual (if indeed we can assume a causal relationship) is likely to vary depending upon a range of factors, many of which are yet to be identified.

SUMMARY AND PLAN OF THE BOOK

In this chapter several topics have been addressed in an effort to place the later discussion of childhood life stress in perspective. One topic related to what is meant by the term "stress." This term has been used in a variety of ways. In some cases it has been used to refer to the experiencing of "stressful" events. In other instances it has been defined in terms of the individual's response to various stimuli. In still other cases "stress" has been defined in terms of person-environment interactions, with an emphasis placed on the role of cognitive appraisal as a primary determiner of the actual stressfulness of events. None of these views has been uniformly accepted by researchers working in the area. Without attempting to arrive at an agreed-upon definition of this construct, one can still profitably focus on those environmental stimuli or situations that represent "potential stressors," their impact on the individual, and the degree to which the impact of these potential stressors is mediated by other variables.

In the adult literature, life stress (defined in some studies as the experiencing of change per se and in others as the experiencing of negative events) is significantly correlated with a range of variables suggestive of health and adjustment difficulties. However, a number of methodological and conceptual issues must be taken into account in interpreting these findings, and conclusions based on this literature (beyond that of concluding there is a general relationship between life stress and health-related variables) must be drawn with a degree of caution.

With this discussion of the concept of stress and brief overview of work in the adult area as background, the remaining chapters deal specifically with life changes experienced by children and adolescents. In the next chapter a range of measures for assessing life changes in younger age groups is considered, with appropriate attention given to assumptions underlying their development and data pertaining to the validity and reliability of these measures. Chapters 3 and 4 will focus on the relationships between cumulative life changes and problems of physical health and psychological adjustment, respectively. These will be followed by a general discussion of conceptual and methodological issues that need to be taken into account when interpreting research findings or conducting research in the area (Chapter 5). The final chapter provides a general overview of research findings and considers priorities for future work in the area, including the need to develop effective programs for helping children and adolescents cope with stressful life changes.

It is intended that the present text serve as an up-to-date overview of work in the area of child/adolescent life stress. It is hoped that the material presented will provide readers with an appreciation of the potential impact of stressful life changes on children and youth, make them aware of the issues that must be dealt with in conducting work in this area, and perhaps stimulate some to pursue work that might enhance our knowledge of the effects of stress on children—despite the practical and methodological issues involved.

2

ASSESSING LIFE EVENTS IN CHILDHOOD AND ADOLESCENCE
A Comparison of Approaches

Despite studies dealing with the effects of specific events or life transitions such as birth of a sibling, divorce, death or a parent, hospitalization, and the like (see Felner, 1984; Felner, Farber, & Primavera, 1980; Felner et al., 1983 for overviews), most life stress investigations have focused on *cumulative* life changes and their relationship to problems of health and adjustment. This emphasis on cumulative change relates to the common assumption that when increased numbers of stressful events are experienced within a relatively short period of time, the person's coping ability is most severely taxed and the person is at greatest risk for developing health-related difficulties (Holmes & Rahe, 1967).

As indicated in the previous chapter, life changes in adults have usually been assessed by using the Schedule of Recent Experiences (Holmes & Rahe, 1967) or variations on this measure, although other scales that provide separate indices of positive and negative change and index the stressfulness of events through self-ratings of event impact have also been developed (Johnson & Sarason, 1979; Sarason et al., 1978) and are being used with increasing frequency.

Measures of child and adolescent life stress have been patterned to a great extent after these adult measures. Although several measures suitable for use with younger age groups are now available, the major differences in approaches to child/adolescent life stress assessment are perhaps best exemplified in the work of Coddington (1972a, 1972b) and of Johnson and his colleagues (Brand & Johnson, 1982; Gad & Johnson, 1980; Johnson, 1982; Johnson & McCutcheon, 1980). In addition to the development of these measures (and others similar to them), some attention has recently been given to the assessment of family life changes and the relationship between these changes, experienced by both parents and child, and health-related variables (McCubbin, Needle, & Wilson, 1985; Patterson & McCubbin, 1983).

This chapter describes the nature of existing measures of child and adolescent life change and considers in some detail what is known regarding the validity, reliability, strengths, and weaknesses of these measures. A more general overview of methodological issues related to life stress assessment is reserved for Chapter 5.

CHILD AND ADOLESCENT
LIFE CHANGE UNIT SCALES

The Coddington Life Stress Scale

The best-known and widely used life stress measure for younger age groups is the Life Events Record, developed by Coddington (1972a). This measure, although designed for children, is similar to the Holmes and Rahe (1967) measure in terms of its construction format, method of scoring, and the assumptions underlying its development.

The Life Events Record consists of a simple listing of events judged to be frequently experienced by children and adolescents. The actual number of events included in the scale varies depending on the age of the child. A preschool version, for example, lists 30 events; an elementary school version, 36 events; a junior high version, 40 events; and a senior high version, 42 events. In completing the measure, parents (in the case of very young children) or children (in the case of those who are old enough to respond to the measure themselves) are requested to indicate which of the events listed have been experienced during the recent past (usually the past year) and the number of times the events have been experienced. As with the adult SRE, life stress scores are derived by summing values termed *life change units* that are associated with the various events that have been experienced. To obtain these life change units, 243 raters (teachers, pediatricians, mental health workers) were initially presented with a list of the events to be included in the measure and were asked to rate each of these with regard to the average amount of social readjustment necessitated by the event. In making these ratings, the event "birth of a sibling" was given an arbitrary value of 500 and raters were asked to give each of the other events a value of above or below 500 to indicate greater or lesser degrees of readjustment. After these ratings were obtained, average readjustment ratings were computed, and life change units were determined by dividing ratings for each event by the constant 10 and rounding out the specific figures. Again, a total life stress score is obtained by adding change units associated with those specific life events that the child has experienced. Examples of events included in the measure at various age levels and their associated life change units are presented in Table 2.1.

In an early study, Coddington (1972b) used this measure to obtain information regarding life change scores obtained by normal children of various ages. The sample consisted of some 3,526 children ranging from preschoolers to those in senior high school who varied in sex, race, and socioeconomic status. From this study it was possible not only to derive normative data for various age groups but also to examine the relationship between the degree of life change experienced and specific demographic variables.

The results of this study suggested a strong relationship between the amount of life change experienced and the age of the child, with older children and adolescents experiencing significantly higher levels of life change than younger children. Based on these group data, Coddington was able to construct a curve (see Figure 2.1), analogous to a growth curve, in which mean life change units (along with standard deviations) are plotted as a function of age. These data are useful in determining whether an individual child has experienced a significantly higher level of life change than normal same-age peers. The study found no relationship between either race or sex and life change scores. However, there was a tendency for subjects from lower socioeconomic groups to show higher levels of life change, a finding that has since been confirmed (Gad & Johnson, 1980) using a different measure of life change.

In addition to the normative data provided in this investigation, data bearing on the validity of the Coddington scale have been provided by a large number of studies investigating the relationship between life change (as assessed by this measure) and indices of child health and adjustment. The results of these studies will be discussed in

TABLE 2.1

Events and Life Change Units for the Coddington Life Events
Record for Use with Four Age Groups

Life Events	Life Change Units			
	Preschool	Elementary	Junior High	Senior High
Beginning nursery school, first grade, or high school	42	46	45	42
Change to a different school	33	46	52	56
Birth or adoption of brother or sister	50	50	50	50
Brother or sister leaving home	39	36	33	37
Hospitalization of brother or sister	37	41	44	41
Death of brother or sister	59	68	71	68
Change of father's occupation requiring increased absence from home	36	45	42	38
Loss of job by parent	23	38	48	46
Marital separation of parents	74	78	77	69
Divorce of parents	78	84	84	77
Hospitalization of parent (serious illness)	51	55	54	55
Death of parent	89	91	94	87
Death of grandparent	30	38	35	36
Marriage of parent to stepparent	62	65	63	63
Jail sentence of parent for 30 days or less	34	44	50	53
Jail sentence of parent for 1 year or more	67	67	76	75
Addition of third adult to family	39	41	34	34
Change in parent's financial status	21	29	40	45
Mother beginning work	47	44	36	26
Decrease in number of arguments between parents	21	25	29	27
Increase in number of arguments between parents	44	51	48	46
Decrease in number of arguments with parents	22	27	29	26
Increase in number of arguments with parents	39	47	46	47
Discovery of being an adopted child	33	52	70	64
Acquiring a visible deformity	52	69	83	81
Having a visible congenital deformity	39	60	70	62
Hospitalization of yourself (child)	59	62	59	58
Change in acceptance by peers	38	51	68	67
Outstanding personal achievement	23	39	45	46
Death of a close friend (child's friend)	38	53	65	63
Failure of a year in school		57	62	56
Suspension from school		46	54	50
Pregnancy of an unwed teen-age sister		36	60	64
Becoming involved with drugs or alcohol		61	70	76
Becoming a member of church/ synagogue		25	28	31

TABLE 2.1   Continued

	Life Change Units			
Life Events	Preschool	Elementary	Junior High	Senior High
Not making an extracurricular activity you wanted to be involved in (i.e., athletic team, band)			49	55
Breaking up with boyfriend/girlfriend			47	53
Beginning to date			55	51
Fathering an unwed pregnancy			76	77
Unwed pregnancy			95	92
Being accepted to a college of your choice				43
Getting married				101

SOURCE: From "The Significance of Life Events as Contributing Factors in the Diseases of Children" by J. S. Heisel, S. Ream, R. Raitz, M. Rappaport, and R. D. Coddington, *Journal of Pediatrics,* 1973, *83,* 119-123. Copyright 1973 *Journal of Pediatrics.* Reprinted by permission.

Chapters 3 and 4; suffice to say that scores derived from this scale have been found to relate to a wide variety of relevant dependent variables. Although such studies provide general support for the validity of the Coddington scale, there is currently little information concerning the reliability of the measure.

Additional Life Change Unit Measures

Several variations on the Coddington scale have also been developed. Monaghan, Robinson, and Dodge (1979) for example, developed a British modification of the Life Events Record: the Children's Life Events Inventory. This 40-item measure was developed using methods similar to those used for the original scale, with some changes in item content. No validity or reliability data for this measure have been reported. Yeaworth, York, Hussey, Ingle, and Goodwin (1980) likewise developed a measure that employs a life change unit approach to assessment, using a 31-item scale composed of events deemed appropriate for an adolescent population. However, unlike the Coddington measure, in this measure life change units were derived by having adolescents themselves rate events rather than rely-

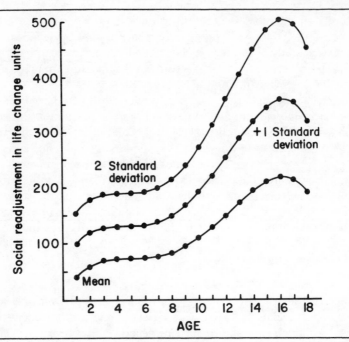

Figure 2.1 Life stress scores at different age levels. Source: Coddington (1972b). Reprinted by permission.

ing on readjustment estimates provided by adults. Although the authors have provided some normative data for a small sample of 207 subjects, no validity or reliability data have been reported. One additional study with this measure has been reported by Ferguson (1981), who used an expanded version of this scale with a small sample (N = 25) of gifted white, suburban ninth graders. This sample of gifted children had lower stress scores on the expanded measure than did a sample of 71 nongifted students, and life change scores were found to be correlated with an index of suicidal ideation.

Finally, Tolor, Murphy, Wilson, and Clayton (1983) developed the High School Social Readjustment Scale specifically for use with adolescents. Estimates of the amount of readjustment associated with each of the 52 events included in the scale were derived by obtaining ratings from 215 psychologists, 67 elementary and high school teachers, and 65 high school students. The authors note that each of these groups was quite similar in terms of their rank ordering of stressful events.

Although the developers of this measure have provided little information on the reliability and validity of the measure, some data provided by a recent study (Tolor & Murphy, 1985) have suggested a significant relationship between scores derived from this measure and indices of depression. Obviously, more data are needed.

Life change unit scales such as those described here have been the most widely used methods of assessing life stress in children and adolescents. Probably as many as 90% of all child life stress studies have employed measures of this type. The Coddington scale, however, appears to be the only one of these measures that is reasonably well supported by research data. As we have seen, normative data have been provided for various age groups, and the validity of the scale has received support from a number of correlational studies documenting significant relationships between Life Event Record scores and indices of health and adjustment. The reliability of this measure, however, has not been established.

Limitations of Life Change Unit Scales

Although the Life Events Record has played an important role in stimulating child life stress research, several limitations of the scale are apparent. The scale provides only an overall measure of life change and makes no distinction between positive and negative life changes. In this respect the Coddington measure is most similar to the adult Schedule of Recent Experiences (Holmes & Rahe, 1967). Underlying the development of both measures is the basic assumption that both positive and negative events require change and social adaptation and are therefore stressful. From this perspective there is no need to consider desirable and undesirable changes separately because it is change per se, rather than the positive or negative aspects of change, that is seen as resulting in stress. Nevertheless, many workers in the area have suggested that life stress can be more adequately conceptualized in terms of events that exert a negative impact on the individual. In fact, studies with adults have suggested that although indices of negative change are found to be consistently correlated with stress-related variables, only negligible relationships are usually found between positive change and relevant dependent measures (Johnson & Sarason, 1979a; Mueller, Edwards & Yarvis, 1977; Sarason et al., 1978; Vinokur &

Selzer, 1975). Although further research on this issue is needed, it may be more appropriate to think of life stress in terms of events that have a negative impact on the individual than in terms of change per se. To the extent that findings in the adult area are applicable to children, the failure to assess positive and negative changes separately is a major limitation of the Coddington scales and similar life event measures.

An additional limitation of the life change unit scales involves the use of life change units in deriving life stress scores. Life change units are purported to provide an index of the amount of change resulting from or the degree of stressfulness associated with experiencing specific events. One might, however, question the extent to which such values actually reflect the amount of stress experienced by children in response to life events. Individuals often vary considerably in their view of events as positive or negative. An event such as a change in residence or moving from one school to another may be viewed as either positive or negative depending on the circumstances surrounding the event and the way in which the event is perceived by the child. Even events such as divorce may be viewed quite differently. One child may appraise the divorce very negatively, perceiving a significant loss; another child, who has had to deal with long-term parental conflict, may view the divorce somewhat more positively. Given that the stressfulness of events most likely depends not simply on their occurrence but on the child's appraisal of them (Lazarus & Folkman, 1985), it seems reasonable to question whether *any* value derived from mean ratings of others can adequately reflect the stressfulness of a specific event for any specific child. Raters employed in deriving life change units for the Coddington scale were asked to provide ratings for all events included on the measure even though they undoubtedly had not even experienced many of these events. And there are recent data to suggest that in some instances adult ratings of life events may not correspond well with children's self-ratings of these same events (Yamamoto & Felsenthal, 1982). Thus for several reasons the sensitivity of life change units as indicators of the stressfulness of events may be called into question.

A further problem with the Coddington scale (and with many of the measures discussed in this chapter) is that it does not provide an adequate sampling of life events experienced by children and adolescents. Lists of events for these scales have typically been derived from the author's experiences with children, with no attempt being made to find out from children which events they actually experience as stressful.

This critique suggests that an optimal measure of child/adolescent life stress should consist of a broad listing of life events including those suggested by children and adolescents themselves. It should provide for the separate assessment of both positive and negative life changes (with the desirability of events perhaps best being indicated by respondents themselves) and should include some more sensitive method for assessing the impact of life change on specific children. Obviously, it is also important to demonstrate that such measures are both reliable and valid.

NON-LIFE CHANGE UNIT MEASURES

Although differing in certain respects, there are several recently developed measures that, to varying degrees, display desirable characteristics such as those just described. These alternative measures are described below.

The Life Events Checklist

Johnson and McCutcheon (1980) developed an alternative life change measure that is suitable for use with older children and adolescents. The Life Events Checklist (presented in Table 2.2) consists of a listing of 46 events along with spaces for respondents to report events not specifically listed. Items were selected by considering items from the Coddington scale, items from adult life change scales (which, in modified form, were judged to be appropriate for use with children and adolescents), and by including items that the authors found to be frequently experienced by children and adolescents. In order to provide for a more adequate sampling of events, a number of additional items were also obtained by conducting an open-ended survey of 44 black and white children and adolescents from varying socioeconomic groups who were asked to list the five most stressful events experienced during the previous year. Thus the measure taps a range of events

TABLE 2.2
The Life Events Checklist

Instructions: Below is a list of things that sometimes happen to people. Put an X in the space by each of the events you have experience during the past year (12 months). For each of the events you check also indicate whether you feel the event has changed or has had an impact or effect on your life by placing a circle around the appropriate statement (no effect—some effect—moderate effect—great effect). Remember, for each event you have experienced during the past year, (1) place an "X" in the space to indicate you have experienced the event, (2) indicate whether you viewed the event as a good or bad event, and (3) indicate how much effect the event has had on your life.

To get some idea of the type of events you will be asked to rate, please read over the entire list before you begin. Only respond to those events you have actually experienced during the past year.

Event	Type of Event (circle one)		Impact or Effect of Event on Your Life			
1. Moving to new home	Good	Bad	no effect	some effect	moderate effect	great effect
2. New brother or sister	Good	Bad	no effect	some effect	moderate effect	great effect
3. Changing to new school	Good	Bad	no effect	some effect	moderate effect	great effect
4. Serious illness or injury of family member	Good	Bad	no effect	some effect	moderate effect	great effect
5. Parents divorced	Good	Bad	no effect	some effect	moderate effect	great effect
6. Increased number of arguments between parents	Good	Bad	no effect	some effect	moderate effect	great effect
7. Mother or father lost job	Good	Bad	no effect	some effect	moderate effect	great effect
8. Death of a family member	Good	Bad	no effect	some effect	moderate effect	great effect
9. Parents separated	Good	Bad	no effect	some effect	moderate effect	great effect
10. Death of a close friend	Good	Bad	no effect	some effect	moderate effect	great effect
11. Increased absence of parent from the home	Good	Bad	no effect	some effect	moderate effect	great effect
12. Brother or sister leaving home	Good	Bad	no effect	some effect	moderate effect	great effect
13. Serious illness or injury of close friend	Good	Bad	no effect	some effect	moderate effect	great effect
14. Parent getting into trouble with law	Good	Bad	no effect	some effect	moderate effect	great effect
15. Parent getting a new job	Good	Bad	no effect	some effect	moderate effect	great effect
16. New stepmother or stepfather	Good	Bad	no effect	some effect	moderate effect	great effect
17. Parent going to jail	Good	Bad	no effect	some effect	moderate effect	great effect
18. Change in parents' financial status	Good	Bad	no effect	some effect	moderate effect	great effect
19. Trouble with brother or sister	Good	Bad	no effect	some effect	moderate effect	great effect
20. Special recognition for good grades	Good	Bad	no effect	some effect	moderate effect	great effect
21. Joining a new club	Good	Bad	no effect	some effect	moderate effect	great effect
22. Losing a close friend	Good	Bad	no effect	some effect	moderate effect	great effect
23. Decrease in number of arguments with parents	Good	Bad	no effect	some effect	moderate effect	great effect

#	Event	Good/Bad	no effect	some effect	moderate effect	great effect
24.	Male: girlfriend getting pregnant	Good Bad	no effect	some effect	moderate effect	great effect
25.	Female: getting pregnant	Good Bad	no effect	some effect	moderate effect	great effect
26.	Losing a job	Good Bad	no effect	some effect	moderate effect	great effect
27.	Making the honor role	Good Bad	no effect	some effect	moderate effect	great effect
28.	Getting your own car	Good Bad	no effect	some effect	moderate effect	great effect
29.	New boyfriend/girlfriend	Good Bad	no effect	some effect	moderate effect	great effect
30.	Failing a grade	Good Bad	no effect	some effect	moderate effect	great effect
31.	Increase in number of arguments with parents	Good Bad	no effect	some effect	moderate effect	great effect
32.	Getting a job of your own	Good Bad	no effect	some effect	moderate effect	great effect
33.	Getting into trouble with police	Good Bad	no effect	some effect	moderate effect	great effect
34.	Major personal illness or injury	Good Bad	no effect	some effect	moderate effect	great effect
35.	Breaking up with boyfriend/girlfriend	Good Bad	no effect	some effect	moderate effect	great effect
36.	Making up with boyfriend/girlfriend	Good Bad	no effect	some effect	moderate effect	great effect
37.	Trouble with teacher	Good Bad	no effect	some effect	moderate effect	great effect
38.	Male: girlfriend having abortion	Good Bad	no effect	some effect	moderate effect	great effect
39.	Female: having abortion	Good Bad	no effect	some effect	moderate effect	great effect
40.	Failing to make an athletic team	Good Bad	no effect	some effect	moderate effect	great effect
41.	Being suspended from school	Good Bad	no effect	some effect	moderate effect	great effect
42.	Making failing grades on report card	Good Bad	no effect	some effect	moderate effect	great effect
43.	Making an athletic team	Good Bad	no effect	some effect	moderate effect	great effect
44.	Trouble with classmates	Good Bad	no effect	some effect	moderate effect	great effect
45.	Special recognition for athletic performance	Good Bad	no effect	some effect	moderate effect	great effect
46.	Getting put in jail	Good Bad	no effect	some effect	moderate effect	great effect
	Other events which have had an impact on your life. List and rate.					
47.	_____	Good Bad	no effect	some effect	moderate effect	great effect
48.	_____	Good Bad	no effect	some effect	moderate effect	great effect
49.	_____	Good Bad	no effect	some effect	moderate effect	great effect
50.	_____	Good Bad	no effect	some effect	moderate effect	great effect

SOURCE: From "Assessing Life Stress in Older Children and Adolescents: Preliminary Findings with the Life Events Checklist" by J. H. Johnson and S. M. McCutcheon in Stress and Anxiety, 1980. Copyright 1980 Hemisphere Publishing. Reprinted by permission.

likely to be experienced by young people. The first 18 events on the scale represent events over which the child is likely to have little personal control and that are unlikely to be confounded with indices of health and adjustment; items 19 to 46 reflect events that are likely to serve as stressors when experienced but that must be viewed as potentially under the control of the individual. Events were divided this way so a distinction could be made between these two broad classes of events when conducting certain types of life stress investigations.

The Life Events Checklist (LEC) yields two values: a positive life change score and a negative life change score. The positive score is derived by summing the impact ratings (0 to 3) of events rated as positive; the negative score by summing the impact ratings (0 to 3) of events rated as negative. A total life change score can also be derived by summing the impact ratings of all events experienced. Although deriving such a score is somewhat redundant (as it is based on positive and negative change scores), it might be desirable to obtain it in some life stress studies. In providing for the separate assessment of positive and negative changes and for individualized rating of the impact of events, this measure is similar to the adult Life Experiences Survey (Johnson & Sarason, 1979a; Sarason et al., 1978).

Preliminary normative data on positive and negative change scores obtained from a sample of 213 male and female subjects drawn from the general population are presented in Table 2.3.

Validity Studies. Although additional research is needed to assess the validity and reliability of the LEC, several studies have yielded data that provide preliminary support for its usefulness. In an early study employing a preliminary version of this scale, Gad and Johnson (1980) found negative life change scores to correlate significantly with a range of variables, including visits to the doctor during the previous year, reports of diagnosed illness, reports of physical health problems, visits to the school counselor, reports of personal problems, and difficulty in coping with personal problems. This study also found a significant relationship between negative change scores and reported drug use. Positive change scores were related to fewer variables. This positive change index was found to be significantly related (in a negative direction) to physician visits (high levels of positive change being associated with fewer visits). Reports of personal problems were positively correlated with the positive change index, but this relationship was much lower than for the index of negative change.

TABLE 2.3
Means and Standard Deviations for Life Events Checklist Scores[a]

Life Events Checklist	All Subjects (N = 213)	Males (N = 134)	Females (N = 79)
Positive change	6.88 (5.74)	6.82 (5.91)	6.97 (5.48)
Negative change	5.46 (5.51)	5.18 (5.30)	5.91 (5.84)

a. Numbers in the top rows are means; numbers in the bottom rows are standard deviations. These data supplied by Judith M. Siegel and Cynthia J. Leitch. (From "Assessing Life Stress in Older Children and Adolescents: Preliminary Findings with the Life Events Checklist" by J. H. Johnson and S. M. McCutcheon in *Stress and Anxiety*, 1980. Copyright 1980 Hemisphere Publishing. Reprinted by permission.)

Johnson and McCutcheon (1980) also examined the relationship between LEC scores and a range of dependent variables, employing a sample of 97 male and female adolescents 13 to 17 years of age. Dependent measures for this study included a short form of the Beck Depression Scale, the Rotter Locus of Control Scale, a measure of trait anxiety (from the State-Trait Anxiety Inventory), and a factor-analytically derived index of emotional maladjustment derived by Johnson and Overall (1973). Additional measures included self-reports of school days missed because of illness, reports of physical health problems, and self-ratings of present and past (previous year) physical health. The relationship between life change scores and scores on a short form of the Marlowe-Crowne Social Desirability Scale was also assessed to determine the degree to which responses to the LEC might be biased by the attempts of subjects to place themselves in a socially acceptable light.

When data from the entire sample were considered, results of this investigation indicated significant correlations between negative change scores and depression, anxiety, emotional maladjustment, and an external locus of control orientation. In each instance, higher levels of negative change were associated with higher levels of depression, anxiety, and so forth. The only significant correlate of positive change scores was locus of control; however, this relationship was in the opposite direction from that found when negative change scores were considered. Here, high levels of positive change were associated with an internal rather than an external locus of control orientation.

Although significant correlations between measures of change and indices of physical health were not found when data from the entire

sample were considered, separate analyses for male and female subjects did uncover some significant relationships. When data for male
subjects were analyzed, significant relationships between negative
change and school days missed as a result of illness, reports of
physical health problems, and ratings of present physical health were
found. A significant negative relationship was also found for males in
that higher levels of positive change were associated with lower levels
of maladjustment. In considering the data for females, no significant
correlations were found between life change scores and indices of physical health. However, significant correlations between measures of
negative changes and indices of maladjustment and external locus of
control were obtained. These findings tentatively suggest that life
stress might relate to different variables in males and females (a finding that needs replication), but most relevant to the current discussion
are findings that measures derived from the Life Events Checklist correlate with a range of relevant dependent variables and that support
was found for the separate assessment of desirable and undesirable
life changes. Support for the discriminant validity of the measure is
suggested by the fact that no significant correlation was found between either of the life change scores and the index of social desirability employed in this study.

In a separate study, Wenet (1979) compared LEC scores obtained
from a group of 25 adolescent male sex offenders with those obtained
from a similar number of adolescents matched for age and sex and
drawn from the general population. No differences were found when
positive change scores were considered. There were, however, significant differences between the groups when the index of negative change
was considered: Negative change scores for the clinical group were
roughly three times those reported by the comparison group.

Further support for the validity of the LEC has been provided by a
study (to be discussed in greater detail later) of some 141 youngsters,
ranging in age from 10 to 17 years, who had juvenile onset or insulin-
dependent diabetes (Brand, Johnson, & Johnson, 1986). In this
investigation, measures of negative life change were found to be
significantly correlated with certain biochemical measures of diabetic
control that have been shown in previous research to be stress related.
Again, no significant correlates of positive life changes were found.
Finally, additional studies by other investigators (see Greene, Walker,
Hickson, & Thompson, 1985; Greenberg, Siegel, & Leitch, 1983;
Smith, Gad, & O'Grady, 1983) have also found scores of the LEC to

correlate significantly with other relevant indices of physical health and psychological adjustment. The nature of these studies will be considered in more detail in later chapters.

Reliability Data. To date, one study of the test-retest reliability of the Life Events Checklist has been reported. In this study (Brand & Johnson, 1982) 50 subjects (ages 10-17), drawn from a university laboratory school, were given the LEC and subsequently retested after a two-week interval. Positive and negative life change scores were obtained by summing the impact ratings of experienced events that were rated desirable and those that were rated undesirable (impact rating procedure), and also by simply summing the numbers of positive and negative events experienced, giving each a weight of 1 (unit rating procedure). Using the simple unit rating procedure, test-retest correlations for positive and negative life change scores were .69 (p < .001) and .72 (p < .001), respectively. When scores were derived using the standard impact rating procedure, test-retest correlations were .71 (p < .001) for positive and .66 (p < .001) for negative change scores. Some events may have actually been experienced between the time of the two testings, so it seems that the Life Events Checklist displays adequate reliability, at least over a two-week interval. This holds true regardless of whether scores are derived from a simple count of positive and negative events experienced or are based on a summing of impact ratings provided by the subject.

Finally, some data regarding the interrater reliability of the LEC have been provided by Gilbert (1985), who had a sample (N = 45) of children and adolescents (ages 11-18) and their mothers both complete this measure by indicating events experienced by subjects during the previous year. Although there was an obvious tendency for mothers to underestimate the number of events experienced (and the impact of these events), significant correlations between child/adolescent and parent reports of events were found. The obtained correlations, when weighted indices of positive and negative change were considered separately, were .48 and .60, respectively.

An Overview. The finding that Life Events Checklist scores are reasonably reliable, that they are uncorrelated with measures of social desirability, that they correlate with a range of relevant dependent measures, and that these scores can differentiate between clinic and nonclinic groups would seem to provide at least preliminary support for the measure. That positive and negative change scores are found to be differentially related (sometimes in opposite directions) to dependent measures suggests that the separate assessment of desirable and undesirable life change provided by this measure may represent a distinct advantage over measures that yield only an overall score.

Several types of studies appear necessary to provide more information concerning the Life Events Checklist. In addition to studies designed to assess the relationship between LEC scores and other stress-related measures, further investigations of the test-retest reliability of the LEC (over longer time periods) and the usefulness of the event-weighting procedure used in scoring are needed. Finally, studies comparing the Life Events Checklist to other child/adolescent life change measures, in the prediction of health and adjustment problems, would be especially useful.

The Junior High Life Experiences Survey

An additional measure that in many ways is patterned after the Life Events Checklist (Johnson & McCutcheon, 1980) and the adult Life Experiences Survey (Johnson & Sarason, 1979a; Sarason et al., 1978) is the Junior High Life Experiences Survey (JHLES) developed by Swearingen and Cohen (1985a).

This measure consists of 39 items (along with spaces to include events not listed) that are similar in content to those included in the measures already discussed. Respondents are asked to report events occurring within the past six months and to rate these events as positive, negative, or neutral. After making these desirability ratings, subjects are asked to rate the impact of these events along a 7-point scale (-3 = very bad change to +3 = very good change). As with the Life Events Checklist, it is possible to derive positive, negative, and total life change scores that are based either on a simple count of the number of events experienced or on the sum of the impact ratings given to experienced events.

Preliminary findings with the JHLES have been provided by studying the relationships between life change measures derived from this scale and dependent variables similar to those employed in previous life stress studies (Swearingen & Cohen, 1985a). In this study, the JHLES was administered, along with the State-Trait Anxiety Inventory for Children and the Child Depression Inventory, to 233 seventh- and eighth-grade males and females. Information was also obtained regarding the number of days of school missed during the most recent grading period. Several life change measures were derived in order to assess the optimal way of weighting events. These included simple counts of the number of positive, negative, and total events experienced as well as positive, negative, and total change scores calculated by summing the impact ratings of those events experienced. The investigators also computed a total life change score by summing social readjustment ratings (similar to Coddington's life change units) associated with each of the events experienced. These values were derived by having a sample of 81 child psychologists rate each of the 39 events with regard to the amount of readjustment required by the event when experienced. The event "new brother or sister" was assigned a value of 50 and was used as the anchor point in rating the other events, in a manner similar to that employed in developing the Coddington measure (Coddington, 1972a).

Measures of negative life change were found to be significantly related to anxiety, depression, and school absences, whereas positive changes were generally unrelated to these measures. Indeed, the only significant correlation with positive change suggested that higher levels of self-rated positive changes were related to *lower* levels of depression. These investigators also found scores based on a simple count of events to be as highly correlated with dependent measures as were those based on impact ratings provided by the subject. Further, negative change scores were generally found to be more highly correlated with dependent measures than scores derived by summing readjustment ratings for the total number of events experienced. Based on these findings, Swearingen and Cohen (1985a) advocated a scoring procedure that involves a simple count of the number of positive and negative events experienced, with the desirability of events being determined by self-ratings.

These findings provide preliminary support for the validity of the JHLES as well as additional data regarding the importance of obtaining separate measures of positive and negative life changes in life stress research. They also are consistent with the findings of Johnson and McCutcheon (1980) with children, as well as several studies with adults (Ross & Mirowski, 1981) that suggest that a simple count of positive and negative events is as predictive of stress-related measures as are scores derived by summing impact ratings. These results are also of interest as they suggest, at least tentatively, that indices of negative change are more predictive of stress-related outcomes than are measures obtained by summing life change unit scores, such as those used with the Coddington scale.

The Adolescent Perceived Events Scale

An additional measure that is in some ways similar to the two described above is the Adolescent Perceived Events Scale (APES; Compas, Davis, Forsythe, & Wagner, 1985). It is similar in that it provides for the separate assessment of desirable and undesirable life change and for the individualized rating of events. It differs from the LEC and the JHLES primarily in that it provides a greater sampling of life events, including the assessment of daily stressors, pleasures, and major life changes.

Scale Development. The initial step in the development of the APES involved surveying some 654 adolescents between the ages of 12 and 17 in order to develop an item pool that would reflect major life events, daily hassles, and pleasures experienced by those in this age group. In this survey, adolescents were provided with an open-ended questionnaire that asked them to list major life events experienced within the past six months and daily hassles and pleasures experienced within this same period. Asking subjects to provide information concerning daily hassles was based on the findings of Kanner et al. (1981) and DeLongis, Coyne, Dakof, Folkman, and Lazarus (1983) with adults, suggesting that many daily events (e.g., being picked on by others, dealing with inconsiderate people, having to wait in line, being stuck in traffic) can be stressful and that measures of daily hassles may be more highly correlated with indices of health and adjustment than are major life events. Obtaining information regarding pleasant events was based on the view that existing measures have inadequately attended to the adaptive significance of positive events (Felner, 1984; Felner et al., 1983), and that such events should be more adequately represented in life change measures. This survey of adolescents resulted in a total of 217 nonredundant events (major events, daily hassles, pleasures), which are included in the final measure.

After the selection of events to be included in the measure, an attempt was made—through the use of multidimensional scaling procedures—to determine those dimensions most commonly employed by adolescents in their appraisal of events. A range of dimensions was initially included in these analyses (e.g., desirable/undesirable, high impact/low impact, controllable/uncontrollable, predictable/unpredictable; generality of cause [cause affects just this event/cause affects many events]), however, only three of these dimensions appeared relevant to the appraisal of events by these subjects (36 male and female adolescents; ages 12-20). These included the desirability dimension, the impact dimension, and the generality of cause dimension (which was found to be of relevance in only one age group). Because the relevance of these dimensions of appraisal varied depending on the age of the subjects, three slightly different versions of the APES were developed. Thus for young adolescents (ages 12-14), events are rated only along the dimension of desirability. With middle adolescents (ages 15-17), events are rated on the dimensions of desirability, impact of event, and globality of cause. In the oldest group (ages 18-20) events are rated on the two dimensions of desirability and impact.

Reliability Data. Test-retest reliability data for a group of older adolescents (college freshmen, ages 17 to 20) has been provided. In this study the older adolescent version of the APES was administered to 51 subjects who were asked to report events occurring during the previous three months. This measure was readministered after a two-week interval. At this time subjects were asked to report events experienced during the same three-month period that had been assessed during the first testing. Several types of reliability data were obtained.

The overall correlation between the total number of events reported at Time 1 and Time 2 was quite significant ($r = .77$; $p < .001$), and percentage agreement for specific events reported at the two testings was .89. (Percentage agreement equals the sum of events reported as occurring at both times plus events reported as not occurring divided by the total number of events.) This latter index of agreement goes beyond simply indexing the correlation between overall *scores* obtained at two points in time; it assesses the degree to which individual events are reported (or not reported) consistently over time. The findings suggest that subjects were quite consistent in their reports.

When events reported as positive and negative were considered separately, adequate levels of reliability were also found. Here correlations between weighted positive and negative scores obtained at Time 1 and Time 2 were .84 (weighted positive) and .74 (weighted negative). The overall percentage agreement score for events rated as positive and negative at both Time 1 and Time 2 was .93. At least with older adolescents reporting events over a limited time period, the APES appears to possess adequate test-retest reliability.

Additional data concerning the interrater reliability of this measure have been provided by having a group (N = 34) of older adolescents (college freshmen) complete the APES and then having either a roommate or a close friend of these subjects also respond to the measure by indicating events that the subject had experienced (and whether events were judged by the subject as desirable or undesirable). Here the percentage agreement for reports of events experienced and not experienced was .82. When the desirability of events was taken into account, percentage agreement for events similarly reported as positive or negative by both respondents was .87.

Life events reported by those responding to this measure are likely to be events that have actually been experienced by subjects rather than the results of inaccurate or an otherwise biased reporting of events.

Validity Data. Preliminary validity data have been provided by relating scores derived from the APES to indices of psychological symptoms, as assessed by the Hopkins Symptom Checklist (Derogatis, Lipman, Rickels, Uhlenhuth, & Covi, 1974), in a sample of older adolescents (high school seniors entering college). Briefly, the Hopkins Symptom Checklist (employed as the dependent measure in this study) is a 58-item self-report measure that yields a Total Symptom Index as well as subscales related to depression, anxiety, obsessive-compulsive characteristics, interpersonal sensitivity, and somatization.

Correlations between indices of life change and Hopkins Symptom Checklist measures suggested that weighted negative events were significantly correlated with each of these dependent measures. Consistent with other studies that have considered positive and negative change separately, weighted positive changes were correlated with fewer variables. Here significant correlations were found only when measures of anxiety and obsessive-compulsive characteristics were considered.

The Adolescent Perceived Events Scale: An Overview. Although still in the process of development, this life change index has a number of desirable characteristics. First, it provides the most extensive listing of life events of any existing adolescent measure. As the events included in the scale were determined by surveying large numbers of adolescents in order to determine events that were most stressful to them, the item content is particularly relevant to this population, thus contributing to face validity. Unlike most other measures, specific attention was also given to the inclusion of events likely to be viewed as positive by adolescent respondents. In addition, preliminary research provides support for the reliability of the measure and suggests that indices of life change, derived from the scale, are significantly related to a range of measures that might be expected to reflect the effects of stress. Developers of the APES have attended to a number of issues relevant to scale development.

Despite its strengths, there are significant issues related to the nature of the measure. One is that many of the findings regarding the reliability and validity of the measure have been obtained with older adolescents. Data on test-retest reliability were all obtained using college freshmen as subjects. Likewise, data regarding the interrater reliability of the measure were obtained from college-age subjects enrolled in introductory psychology courses. In addition, validity data in the form of correlations between APES scores and Hopkins Symptom Checklist scores were obtained from older adolescents (high school seniors in the process of entering college). This heavy reliance on data obtained from older adolescents means that at this time we have relatively little information regarding the validity and reliability of the measure with much younger adolescents, who are perhaps those most likely to be included in adolescent life-stress studies. Studies designed to provide such data on younger subjects are currently under way (Compas, 1986).

Although the attempt to determine the most relevant dimensions for rating events through the use of multidimensional scaling techniques is commendable, and although at least one of the dimensions demonstrated to be important in these analyses (e.g., desirability of events) proved to be important in previous research (Johnson & McCutcheon, 1980; Swearingen & Cohen, 1985a), these findings must be interpreted cautiously. Multidimensional scaling analyses were accomplished with a relatively small sample (N = 36) of adolescents selected to represent three age groups (e.g., 12-14, 15-17, 18-20). Only one-third of this total sample was represented in each of these age groups. Consequently, findings from these analyses need to be replicated before major conclusions can be drawn regarding the most relevant dimensions of appraisal for adolescents of different ages. Because the dimensions of desirability and impact were found to be important for two of the three groups, these dimensions are likely to be replicable. The importance of the generality of cause dimension is less clear. In any event, more research seems necessary before it is concluded that three separate measures are needed to assess events across adolescence.

Finally, although the present measure shows adequate reliability for events reported over a three-month period (at least for college students), reliability data for events assessed over a longer time span would be desirable. Recall of events over a longer period of time may be impaired, but the fact that many life event studies focus on events occurring over a much longer period (e.g., 12 months) makes these kinds of data especially relevant. Despite the fact that more information regarding issues such as these is needed, the Adolescent Perceived Events Scale represents one of the more well-developed measures available for use with older adolescent populations.

ASSESSING FAMILY LIFE EVENTS

Rather than focusing exclusively on adult or child/adolescent life stress, some attention has recently been given to the assessment of family stressors. This focus has developed from the view that the family is a social system made up of interconnected members and from the related assumption that all events affecting one member affect other family members as well. As suggested by Patterson and McCubbin (1983, p. 257), "Life events, both normative and situational, which are experienced by the family as a whole or by any one member are ... added together to determine the magnitude of life change for a family. It is expected that cumulative family life changes will be associated with a decline in family functioning and with negative correlates in individual members."

To provide a measure of family-related stressors suitable for use with adolescents, McCubbin, Patterson, Bauman, and Harris (1982) developed the Adolescent-Family Inventory of Life Events and Changes (A-FILE). This measure is composed of 50 self-report items designed to assess life events and changes experienced by members of the adolescent's nuclear family. Item content reflects family-related events similar to those found in existing adult and child life event measures. Also included are events often experienced by families as a result of moving through different stages of the family life cycle. Both positive and negative events are included, as all are assumed to require a degree of readjustment in the regular pattern of interaction among family members. Examples of events included within each of the six categories that make up the measure are presented in Table 2.4.

Scoring of the A-FILE involves obtaining a simple unweighted sum of the total number of events experienced, with no distinction being made between desirable and undesirable events. Originally, an attempt was made to use weights similar to those derived by Coddington (1972a) and Holmes and Rahe (1967); however, these proved to be no more useful than the simpler unit rating procedure.

Limited information is available regarding the validity and reliability of this measure, but normative data (on 500 male and female junior and senior high school students) along with some preliminary reliability and validity findings have been provided. The authors report an initial test-retest reliability study in which scores were obtained on 74 junior and senior high school students at two points, separated by a two-week interval. A test-retest coefficient of .84 was obtained. The authors note that overall scores derived from this scale have been found to correlate with variables such as health locus of control (Wallston, Wallston, & DeVellu, 1978), high levels of stress being associated with lowered perceptions of control over health-related behaviors. Likewise, McCubbin et al. (1985) have found A-FILE scores to be significantly correlated with adolescent substance abuse, as indicated by reports of cigarette smoking, marijuana smoking, and alcohol use. (Appropriately, A-FILE items related to substance abuse were deleted in these analyses.) A measure similar to this (the Family Inventory of Life Events and Changes [FILE]—Patterson & McCubbin, 1983), developed for use with other family members, has also been found to correlate significantly with child health status when used with families having a chronically ill child (e.g., cystic fibrosis). Scores from this measure also have been shown to correlate significantly with general measures of family functioning

TABLE 2.4
Example of Events Included in the A-FILE

Transitions (14 items)
　　Parents separated or divorced
　　Family moved to new home

Losses (7 items)
　　Parent died
　　Death of close friend or family member

Responsibilities and Strains (19 items)
　　Parent(s) and teenager(s) have increased arguments (hassles) over choice of
　　friends and/or social activities
　　Increase in parent's time away from family
　　Family member ran away

Legal Conflict (2 items)
　　Family member was robbed or attacked (physically or sexually)
　　Family member went to jail, juvenile detention, or was placed on court probation

Sexuality (4 items)
　　Unmarried family member became pregnant
　　Family member had abortion

Substance Abuse (4 items)
　　Family member drinks too much alcohol

SOURCE: Adapted from McCubbin, Patterson, Bauman, and Harris (1982) and reprinted by permission.

(e.g., cohesion, independence, organization, conflict), as assessed by the Moos (1976) Family Environment Scales.

Despite limited data regarding the validity of the A-FILE, findings related specifically to this measure, when considered along with those obtained with the FILE (which is similar in format), seem to provide at least tentative support for the usefulness of family-based life event measures. Clearly, additional research is needed.

SUMMARY

Several measures designed to assess life events experienced by children, adolescents, and families have been discussed in this chapter. These measures have been based on different assumptions regarding the nature of life stress and have employed different approaches to assessing and quantifying the impact of life change on the child.

Representative of existing approaches are the Coddington Life Events Record, the Life Events Checklist, and the Adolescent-Family Inventory of Life Events and Changes. Based on the assumption that life events are stressful regardless of their desirability, the Coddington measure provides an overall index of life change derived by summing values, termed *life change units*, associated with each of the events experienced. The Life Events Checklist, in contrast, provides for the separate assessment of desirable and undesirable life changes as these are perceived by the child. Also, instead of using life change units to index the impact of events, subjects themselves provide individualized ratings of the impact of events they have experienced (a somewhat similar approach has also been taken in the development of the Junior High Life Experiences Survey and the Adolescent Perceived Events Scale. The Family Inventory of Life Events and Changes has been developed in a manner similar to the Coddington scale but focuses on family life events rather than life events more specifically related to one's child or adult status.

Although additional studies of the validity and reliability of these measures (and others similar to them) are clearly needed, research findings suggesting that it is primarily negative change that is correlated with problems of health and adjustment suggest that measures providing for the separate assessment of desirable and undesirable life changes may be superior to those yielding only a single index of life change. In this respect, the Life Events Checklist (and other similar measures) may provide useful ways of assessing stressful life changes in children and adolescents. Nevertheless, research in the area of child life stress assessment is still in its infancy, and there are many issues regarding the sampling of events, the weighting of event impact, the timing of assessment, and other aspects of the procedure that remain to be addressed. A number of these assessment issues will be considered in greater detail in Chapter 5.

3

LIFE EVENTS AND PHYSICAL HEALTH

Much of the adult literature on stress has focused on the relationship between cumulative life changes and the development of physical health problems. Although there are fewer studies with children than with adults, the publication of child life event studies dealing with health-related variables has increased dramatically in recent years. Some of these studies have focused on stressful life changes and accident rates. Some have studied the relationship between life changes and general illness indicators. Others have considered the relationship between life change and the onset of specific health problems. Still others have dealt with the relationship between life changes and health status in children with chronic illnesses of various types. This chapter reviews the physical health correlates of child/adolescent life stress suggested by the results of these investigations. The relationship of life changes to problems of a psychological nature is considered separately in Chapter 4.

Because the majority of studies dealing with the psychological and physical health correlates of child and adolescent life stress are characterized by methodological inadequacies (e.g., retrospective reporting of life events, self-reports of health/adjustment problems, confounding of independent and dependent variables, and so forth), a detailed critique of individual studies will not be presented at this point, although specific evaluative comments are included when judged to be especially pertinent. A more general discussion of methodological issues relevant to this area is presented in Chapter 6.

LIFE STRESS AND ACCIDENT FREQUENCY

The fact that accidents are a major cause of death among children and adolescents (as well as adults) has resulted in researchers becoming interested in those factors that may contribute to accidental injuries in children. Several studies have considered life stress as a possible contributor. In one such study, Padilla, Rohsenow, and Bergman (1976) explored the relationship between life stress and accident frequency in a sample of 103 seventh-grade boys drawn from the general population. Subjects were asked to complete a modified version of the Coddington scale, with life stress scores being obtained by summing life change units for events experienced within the past 12 months. Children who scored in the upper and lower 27% of the distribution of life stress scores were selected for further study.

As the study was prospective in nature, subjects were interviewed weekly over a five-month period by research assistants to obtain information about the occurrence and severity of any accidents they experienced. All interviewers were blind with regard to the subjects' life stress scores. Results of this study suggested that boys who had experienced higher levels of life change reported having significantly more accidents than did boys with low life change scores.

Life stress scores were also found to be a stronger predictor of accident frequency than was an index of "risk taking," which the investigators had predicted would also be related to accident frequency.

Although this study might be faulted on the grounds that self-report measures of accident frequency were employed, its prospective nature and the fact that interviewers were blind with regard to subjects' group membership make it a relatively well-designed investigation (compared to many in the child literature) and increase the likelihood of real differences between the groups.

In a second investigation, Beautrais, Fergusson, and Shannon (1982) studied the relationship between life changes experienced within the family and childhood morbidity in 1,265 children between the ages of 1 and 4 years. In this study major life changes experienced during the child's first four years of life were obtained through the use of a modified version of the Holmes and Rahe scale. Also obtained was information regarding visits with general practitioners, hospital attendance, and hospital admissions for several types of illnesses as well as for accidental poisoning, burns and scalds, and other accidents (e.g., lacerations, bruising, fractures), and suspect home conditions. These investigators found increased levels of family stress to be associated with an increased frequency of accidents of various types as well as with suspect home conditions and the development of various types of physical problems (respiratory illness, gastrointestinal illness). The authors noted that there was a general trend for morbidity rates to increase in direct proportion to the amount of stress experienced. Indeed, children from families who experienced 12 or more life events were found to be, on the average, six times more likely to have been hospitalized than were children from families with three or fewer life events. Children whose families had experienced higher levels of life stress were also more likely to have been seen by a private practitioner for problems such as those considered in this study or to have had contact with a hospital on an outpatient basis. It is especially noteworthy that the significant relationships between stress and child morbidity were found even after controlling for variables such as maternal age, ethnic status, educational level, family size, and so forth, thus decreasing the likelihood that the results can be accounted for by extraneous variables.

In a final study that dealt specifically with accidental athletic injuries, Coddington and Troxell (1980) obtained life stress scores (for the previous 12 months) on 114 high school football players and then followed these students to determine the frequency of their athletic injuries during the subsequent football season. Those students who experienced events such as parental illnesses, separations, divorces, and deaths in the family were found to be more likely to sustain significant athletic injuries than those who had not experienced such events. This finding is similar to those obtained by Bramwell et al. (1975), who found that among college football players, major injuries were related to the level of life events experienced. Findings such as these suggest a general relationship between the amount of stress experienced by the child, adolescent, and/or family and accidental injuries of various types. These findings, taken together, suggest that one effect of stress might be a reduction of parental or personal vigilance that leads to ignoring relevant environmental cues that, if appropriately processed, might have helped prevent these accidents.

LIFE STRESS AND SPECIFIC
HEALTH-RELATED CONDITIONS

Although it did not employ life stress measures such as those emphasized here, one of the earliest studies of life stress and childhood illness was published almost 25 years ago (Meyer & Haggerty, 1962). In this pioneering study, 100 children were followed prospectively for a period of 12 months; throat cultures for streptococcal infections were taken from each child every two weeks. The family members were asked to keep a diary of "upsetting" events encountered by family members during this time and to record any illnesses that were experienced. The results suggested that the two weeks preceding streptococcal infections were generally marked by an increased level of upsetting events and that these were correlated with clinical manifestations of upper respiratory tract illness. Although not all infections were preceded by upsetting events (clearly suggesting that streptococcal infections can occur in the absence of stressful events), the investigators found that the probability of infection significantly increased when stressful events *were* experienced (tentatively suggesting that upsetting events may contribute to the development of this particular variety of illness).

Another early study by Heisel, Ream, Raitz, Rappaport, and Coddington (1973) also served to set the stage for later investigations focusing on the link between stressful life changes and child health. In this investigation, Heisel et al. obtained life stress scores on several groups of children with a variety of physical health difficulties. Included were 34 children with juvenile rheumatoid arthritis, 31 children hospitalized for appendectomies or herniorrhaphies, 32 children admitted to a children's hospital general pediatric service for a range of physical complaints, and 35 children diagnosed as having hemophilia. Children in each of the first three groups were assessed (using the Coddington Life Events Record) with regard to the amount of life stress experienced during the year preceding admission. For the children with hemophilia, the relationship between the number of hemorrhages and life events that accrued during each year of a two-year period was examined. When life event scores of children in the rheumatoid arthritis, general pediatric, and surgery groups were individually compared to life stress scores obtained by a normative sample of healthy children (Coddington, 1972b), each of these groups was found to display significantly higher life event scores. When the children with hemophilia were considered, a relationship was also found between life stress scores and hemorrhagic episodes, although this relationship was attenuated when the frequent hospitalizations experienced by these children were discounted (Coddington, 1979). The authors interpreted the results of this study as providing tentative support for a relationship between stressful life change and the development of childhood illness. In addition to these findings, a number of subsequent studies have also provided support for a relationship between life change and specific physical conditions of childhood and adolescence. The results of these studies are discussed below.

Adolescent Pregnancy

Although it is not considered an illness, pregnancy in adolescence does, in some cases, have significant physical as well as social implications because it increases the health risk to both mother and child. Given an increase in the frequency of teenage pregnancies in recent years (U.S. Department of Health, Education and Welfare, 1976), many investigators have sought to determine factors that may contribute to pregnancy in this age group. One study, designed to assess the possible role of life stress, has been published by Coddington (1979).

In this study information regarding the amount of life stress experienced over a 12-month period (which covered events occurring up to seven to ten months before conception) was obtained from 121 pregnant adolescents who ranged in age from 14 to 19 years. Similar information was obtained on a sample of 261 nonpregnant adolescent girls, who served as the study's control group. Comparisons of these groups in terms of overall level of life stress indicated that pregnant adolescents showed significantly higher levels of recent life change than did those in the comparison group. Especially noteworthy were differences with regard to life events occurring within the family over which the adolescent had little or no control. Pregnant adolescents reported death or illness of a parent, death of a grandparent, and separation of parents more often than did nonpregnant adolescents. There was a nonsignificant trend for this group to reporting the death of a sibling more often than did nonpregnant females.

An additional aspect of this study involved only those who were pregnant and focused on determining the relationship between life stress and obstetric complications. Here, information related to problems of pregnancy and delivery was obtained on 55 cases by inspecting delivery room records. No relationship was found between extent of life change experienced and complications. The author notes that this finding is perhaps not unexpected, given that research with adults by other investigators (Nuckolls et al., 1972) has suggested that the link between life stress and complications of pregnancy and delivery may be mediated by other variables, such as the level of social support or degree of psychosocial assets displayed by the expectant mother, women with high life stress and low levels of support being at greatest risk. Given that potential moderators of this relationship were not assessed in this study, it is possible that stress may have been related to complications in some undetermined subset of this adolescent sample, even in the absence of a significant overall correlation.

At first glance, the findings of significant differences between pregnant and nonpregnant adolescents seem to suggest a link between life stress, particularly family-related stressors, and adolescent pregnancy. Unfortunately, demographic data provided by the author suggest significant group differences in terms of both race and socioeconomic status. Thus black females were overly represented among pregnant teenagers, as were those from lower socioeconomic groups. Given research findings suggesting that black adolescents are likely to experience higher levels of life stress (negative life changes) and that life stress appears to be negatively correlated with socioeconomic variables (see Gad & Johnson, 1980), the failure to control for such variables represents a significant limitation of this study. Increased levels of life stress *and* pregnancy may both be related to sociodemographic differences rather than in any sort of causal manner. Other research designed to study life stress and adolescent pregnancy while controlling for such variables is needed. Likewise, additional research with adolescents that considers life stress in relation to pregnancy and birth complications along with potential moderators of this relationship is in order.

Recurrent Pain

Several recent studies have considered the impact of life changes on the problem of recurrent pain in children and adolescents. For example, Pantel and Goodman (1983) studied 100 adolescents presenting symptoms of recurrent chest pain at a medical school adolescent clinic. Using items from the Coddington measure as the basis for interviewing subjects about recent negative life events, these investigators found that 31% of the subjects reported the occurrence of "significant negative events" within six months of the onset of their pain. Unforunately, the study did not include a control group, and specific life change scores for the recurrent pain group were not reported.

A more adequately controlled study was conducted by Hodges, Kline, Barbero and Flanery (1984) in which 30 children (11 males, mean age 10 years; 19 females, mean age 11 years) who met specific diagnostic criteria for functional chronic abdominal pain (recurrent pain without a discernible physical basis) were selected from among consecutive referrals to a pediatric gastroenterologist. Two additional groups of children were selected for purposes of comparison. One consisted of 67 consecutive referrals to an outpatient psychiatric service. The other group consisted of volunteers from the general population who had no history of recurrent abdominal pain or psychiatric treatment. Children in each of these groups were administered the Coddington Life Events Record and their parents, a modified version of the Schedule of Recent Experiences (Holmes & Rahe, 1967), as well as several additional life event items taken from the Sarason et al. (1978) Life Experiences Survey. Life events were reported retrospectively for the previous 12-month period (with current hospitalization not included as a life event).

Comparisons of life stress scores for these three groups indicated that children with recurrent abdominal pain displayed significantly higher life stress scores than children in the healthy control group (as did children in the psychiatric sample). The authors noted that both of these groups obtained life stress scores that were one to two standard deviations above the normative mean for 10-year-olds, as reported by Coddington (1972b). No differences were found with regard to overall parental life stress scores, however.

A final study dealing with the relationship of life stress to recurrent abdominal and chest pain was conducted by Greene et al. (1985). In this study the Johnson and McCutcheon Life Events Checklist was routinely administered to 172 adolescents (ages 11-19) who were seen as patients in a university medical center adolescent clinic. Based on a complete medical history, physical examination, and laboratory findings, patients were classified into six diagnostic groups: (1) those who simply received a routine checkup; (2) those who had acute minor illnesses (without abdominal or chest pain); (3) those with abdominal pain, chest pain, or headaches that had a clinically diagnosed physical cause; (4) those who had recurrent abdominal pain, chest pain, or headache without an identifiable organic cause; (5) those with behavioral problems; and (6) those displaying stable chronic illnesses of various kinds.

When positive and negative life change measures were considered, several differences were found. There were no differences between any of the groups in terms of measures of positive change. However, those patients displaying recurrent pain (without an identifiable physical cause) and those displaying behavior difficulties as primary symptoms were found to differ from all other groups with regard to the amount of negative change experienced. These findings are quite consistent with those obtained by Hodges et al. (1984) in suggesting a significant relationship between life stress and recurrent pain (without organic cause) displayed by children and adolescents. In considering the findings of their study, Greene et al. (1985, p. 22) suggest that life stress measures such as the Life Events Checklist may represent an "efficient, low-cost tool to aid the practitioner in dealing with the broad range of problems seen in adolescence," and that the use of such measures with children displaying functional pain and behavioral problems is important in emphasizing to both parent and child that psychological factors are being considered in the search for the etiology of their problem.

Respiratory Illness

Boyce et al. (1973) provided data regarding the relationship between life stress and childhood respiratory illness. Subjects in this study were 58 children (mean age 4.3 years) who attended a day care/ elementary school center. As part of a larger study, each of these children was assessed five days a week for one year to obtain clinical and laboratory data concerning the presence and severity of respiratory tract illness. Specifically, four dependent variables were considered: number of illnesses, average duration of illness, average severity of illness, and a composite sickness score. After one year, the parents of these children were interviewed to assess retrospectively the degree of life stress experienced during the study period. Life stress was assessed using the Coddington scale.

Life change scores were positively correlated with both the average duration and average severity of illness, but not with number of illnesses. Additional multiple regression analyses, which focused on the relationship between life stress and dependent measures while controlling for several potentially confounding variables (e.g., sex, race, age, family size), also provided support for an association between life stress and these variables.

Of special interest is the fact that children included in the study were also classified as coming from families characterized by high or low attention to routine. Thus in some families there was an emphasis on such routines as getting up at a certain time, eating meals at a particular time, going to bed at a specific time, and so forth. In some families there was little attention to such routines. Analyses of the joint relationships among life stress, adherence to family routine, and illness were found to provide support for the combined effects of the predictor variables (stress and family routines) when the index of illness severity was considered. These results suggested that children who experienced high levels of stress and strongly routinized families were most likely to be characterized by increased severity of illness scores. Thus it seems that life stress itself is a predictor of respiratory illness duration, whereas severity of illness can be predicted best by considering the joint effects of life change and adherence to family routines. These findings not only provide some support for an association between child life stress and respiratory problems but also highlight a point to be considered later: namely, the need for life stress studies to consider the role of variables that may mediate the impact of life changes. Although degree of family routine emerged as a significant moderator variable, its role in the stress-illness relationship was not as originally predicted. The initial hypothesis of the study was that the relationship between life stress and respiratory illness would be attenuated given adherence to a high level of family routine. Thus family routines were assumed to play a stress-buffering role. In fact, the results suggest just the opposite: High life stress in a highly routinized family seems to increase the severity of respiratory problems. The reasons for the apparent interaction of life stress and this particular family variable are unclear, and the role of family structure and its relationship to coping with stress appears worthy of further investigation.)

Childhood Cancer

A final example of studies relating life changes to specific forms of childhood illness has been provided by Jacobs and Charles (1980). This investigation of the relationship between life stress and childhood cancer was an outgrowth of earlier studies by Green and his associates (Green, 1952, 1954; Green, Young, Swisher, & Miller, 1955). Among other findings, these investigators had found that 31 of 33 pediatric patients with leukemia experienced major losses or separations in the two years preceding the onset of their illness. Half of these losses were reported to have occurred during the six months before onset of their disease.

The Jacobs and Charles study was designed to explore this relationship in a somewhat better-controlled manner by comparing life stress scores of child cancer patients with those of a matched control group. Included in the study were 25 children diagnosed as having leukemia, lymphoma, or another malignancy. A comparison group, drawn from a general pediatric clinic, consisted of an equal number of children matched for age, sex, and socioeconomic status. These children displayed a range of generally less serious physical complaints such as sore throat and respiratory infection. Life events experienced by the family, and thus presumably affecting the child, were assessed by having the parents (retrospectively) complete the Schedule of Recent Experiences (Holmes & Rahe, 1967) with regard to events experienced by the child and his or her family during the year prior to illness onset.

When these two groups of children were compared in terms of total life change unit scores, a mean score of 197 was found for the child cancer group compared to a mean score of only 91.8 for the comparison group; this difference was found to be highly significant. A comparison of the number of events experienced, as opposed to life change unit scores, indicated that the child cancer group experienced approximately twice the number of events experienced by control subjects. In addition to focusing on the relationship between cumulative life change scores and childhood cancer, these authors also focused on specific events that were found more often in the recent histories of children with cancer than in children drawn from the general pediatric population. Among these events were marital separations, death of a close family member (52% of the children in the child cancer group had experienced parental separation or loss during the past year, compared to 16% of the control group), change in residence (72% in the child cancer group versus 24% in the control group), change in schools (52% versus 32%), change in health of family member (60% versus 24%), change in number of arguments between family members (20% versus 4%), and others. Thus the study suggests not only that child cancer patients differ from controls in terms of overall life stress but also that they differ to some extent in terms of specific events experienced.

Although the findings obtained here cannot be construed as evidence of a causal relationship between family life stress and childhood cancer (and there are problems in determining precisely the time of illness onset in this type of disorder—a factor that could have influenced life stress scores), these findings are suggestive and further studies in this area are in order.

LIFE STRESS AND ITS RELATIONSHIP
TO CHRONIC ILLNESS

The studies presented to this point have dealt primarily with the association between life events and *onset* of physical illness. Also of interest is the degree to which cumulative life changes relate to fluctuating health status in children and adolescents with chronic illnesses. Although such studies with children are just beginning to appear, there are several studies with adults that are relevant to this issue. For example, at least one adult study has found a relationship between life stress and symptom severity in individuals with asthma (de Araujo et al., 1973). Research by Grant, Kyle, Teichman, and Mendels (1974) and Bradley (1979) has also suggested that life stress may be related to difficulties in diabetic control, at least among those with juvenile-onset diabetes. Finally, recent research by Watson (1983) has suggested a relationship between level of negative life changes and recurrent lesions in individuals with genital herpes. There are relatively few child studies of life stress and chronic illness; however, those that have been reported provide general support for the view that stress may exacerbate the manifestations of physical illness.

In one child study, Bedell, Giordani, Amour, Tavormina, and Boll (1977) studied 45 children attending a three-week summer camp for the chronically ill who displayed a range of illnesses such as diabetes, asthma, and cystic fibrosis. The children were given the Coddington Life Events Record (along with certain personality measures), and camp counselors, who were unaware of the children's life stress scores, were asked to record each time children displayed evidence of any physical health problem that was related to their particular illness while at camp.

Comparisons between children with high and low levels of life stress indicated that those in the high-stress group showed significantly more illness episodes related to their health problems than did children with low stress scores. In fact, during the three-week period during which illness episodes were assessed, children with high life stress scores experienced 69 illness-related episodes, compared to only 19 experienced by children with low levels of stress. Unfortunately, no information was provided to indicate which of the various illnesses displayed by these children (e.g., diabetes, asthma, cystic fibrosis) were most highly related to illness episodes while at camp, and no information was provided regarding the degree to which "illness-related episodes" could be reliably assessed by those making such ratings. Despite the positive results, these factors make it necessary to view these findings with caution.

Several studies have provided data regarding the relationship between specific life events and juvenile-onset diabetes in children. Stein and Charles (1971), for example, found that children with diabetes displayed a significantly higher incidence of parental loss and serious family disturbance than a comparison group of children with other types of chronic illness. This relationship between parental loss and childhood diabetes has also been studied by Leaverton, White, McCormick, Smith, and Sheikholislam (1980). Subjects for this study were 121 children below 18 years of age who had insulin-dependent diabetes and 37 control children matched for age, sex, race, and socioeconomic status who were drawn from the general population. Parents of these children were interviewed to obtain data on parental loss as well as other stressors. When diabetic and control children were compared for occurrence of parental loss (through separation, divorce, or death) before onset of diabetes, a significant relationship was found; parental loss was reported to have occurred in 42% of the families of children with diabetes and in only 19% of the families of control children. The authors interpreted these findings as suggesting that "parental loss due to divorce, separation, or death may be one of several antecedent factors in the development of juvenile diabetes" (p. 658), although it is clear that a causal relationship between parental loss and diabetes onset cannot be inferred from such results.

Two child studies (Brand et al., 1986; Chase & Jackson, 1981) also focused on the relationship between cumulative life changes of various types and control of juvenile-onset diabetes. In the Chase and Jackson study, 84 children and adolescents with insulin-dependent diabetes mellitus were administered an appropriate version of the Coddington life stress measure during routine clinic visits. Life events were assessed (retrospectively) over the previous three months, which generally covered the time since the child's last clinic appointment. A variety of biochemical and clinical measures, reflective of the degree to which the subject's diabetes was under control, were obtained within this same three-month period. Life stress was found to be significantly correlated with a number of dependent measures, such as triglyceride concentrations, cholesterol values, and serum glucose concentrations. Children with elevated Hemoglobin A1 values (a measure considered to be a cumulative index of blood sugar levels over the past three months) were likewise found to have higher life stress scores than those with more clinically normal values. Finally, life stress scores of children who had one or more hospitalizations for ketoacidosis during the previous three months were found to be significantly higher than for children who had not been hospitalized. Here the average score for those requiring hospitalization was 208 life change units, whereas those not requiring hospitalization had an average life change score of only 122. Although this study provided general support for some relationship between life stress and diabetic control, the results were found to hold only for older subjects in the sample—that is, those in the 15- to 18-year age range.

In the Brand et al. (1986) study, the relationship between life stress and diabetic control was investigated with 141 children and adolescents (ages 10-17) attending a two-week diabetes summer camp. Life stress measures for the year preceding camp were obtained via the Johnson and McCutcheon (1980) Life Events Checklist, and a number of measures generally agreed to be reflective of diabetic control were obtained while the child was at camp. These included blood and urine sugar levels, Hemoglobin A1, and an index of urine ketone levels (which provided an indirect measure of the breakdown of body fats). In addition to these measures, all subjects were requested to complete a children's locus of control measure to assess the degree to which the relationship between life stress and diabetic control might vary dependent on the child's perception of control over his or her environment. The inclusion of this measure was prompted by some findings in the adult area suggesting that life stress may have a more adverse impact on individuals who perceive themselves as having little control over their environment (Johnson & Sarason, 1979b). The relationship between life stress and diabetic control was also assessed as a function of both sex and age of the child. Variables thought to possibly confound these relationships (e.g., socioeconomic variables, duration of diabetes) were statistically controlled in the analyses.

When measures of both positive and negative life change were considered, no relationship between positive change and any index of diabetic control was found. Negative life changes, however, were found to be significantly correlated with urine ketone levels. This relationship was found to hold primarily for younger rather than older children, males as opposed to females, and internally as opposed to externally oriented subjects, as indexed by the child locus of control measure. No relationships between life-change scores and blood and urine sugar measures were found.

Although life stress in this study was found to be correlated with fewer measures than in the Chase and Jackson (1981) investigation, the results do provide support for a relationship between life changes and at least some aspects of diabetic control. Further, this study suggests that it is primarily negative changes that are related to indices of control, and that (to the extent that a causal relationship exists) the effects of stress on diabetic control in children may vary as a function of the age and sex of the child and perhaps as a function of the degree to which the child perceives himself or herself as capable of exerting control over the environment. Regarding the locus of control variable, it is noteworthy that it was with internals rather than externals that the strongest relationship between negative change and ketone levels was found. In attempting to account for these unpredicted findings, the authors speculate that for patients who believe they are capable of exerting a degree of environmental control (as should be characteristic of internals), experiencing life changes that truly are outside their control (e.g., parental divorce, death of a parent) may actually be more stressful than if the events had been seen as clearly uncontrollable.

In another study related to chronic childhood illness, Smith, Gad, and O'Grady (1983) investigated the relationship between life stress (as indexed by the Johnson & McCutcheon Life Events Checklist) and health status in a small sample of 26 adolescents (mean age 15 years) with cystic fibrosis. Overall, these patients reported life stress scores that did not differ significantly from scores obtained by subjects from the general population. Based on measures of pulmonary function, X-ray findings, and a rating of the patient's overall condition, it was possible to classify each patient according to the degree of impairment exhibited. When patients were classified in terms of severity of impairment, patients showing greater impairment displayed life stress scores that were significantly higher than those with milder levels of impairment. These differences were found only for measures of negative life change and were found regardless of whether negative change scores were based on a simple count of the number of negative events or on a sum of the impact ratings associated with the negative events experienced. Somewhat similar findings have been obtained by Patterson and McCubbin (1983), who found increased levels of life stress experienced by the family to be related to pulmonary function in children with cystic fibrosis.

SOME ADDITIONAL FINDINGS

Several other studies have explored the relationship between life change and indices of child health and illness using more general dependent measures. For example, Gad and Johnson (1980) found that measures of negative life change were significantly correlated with variables such as number of visits to the doctor, reports of diagnosed illness, and self-reports of physical health problems. Johnson and McCutcheon (1980) also found that, at least with male subjects, life stress was significantly correlated with number of school days missed because of illness, reports of physical health problems, and self-ratings of physical health. Finally, Hotaling, Atwell, and Linsky (1978), using the senior high school version of the Coddington Life Events Record, examined the relationship between life stress and two dependent measures: number of illnesses over 12 months and ratings of physical health during the study period (based on number of illnesses and degree of incapacitation). Life stress scores were found to be significantly related to seriousness of illness, although no relationship was found when number of illnesses was used as the dependent measure. Further examination of the data by assessing the differential relationship between measures of positive and negative life change and seriousness of illness suggested that the previously obtained relationship was primarily attributable to the effects of negative change, given that only the negative change measure was found to relate significantly to the seriousness of illness index.

SUMMARY

This chapter reviewed a number of studies bearing on the relationship between life stress and physical health problems of children and adolescents. In the studies presented, support was found for a relationship between life stress experienced by both the child and family and the frequency of accidents of various types. Other studies suggested a relationship between cumulative life changes and a range of physical problems such as juvenile rheumatoid arthritis, recurrent abdominal pain, functional chest pain, childhood cancer, and the duration and severity of childhood respiratory illness. Still other studies suggested that life stress may be related to the health status of children with chronic illnesses such as diabetes, cystic fibrosis, and perhaps other chronic health problems as well. Finally, data were presented that are supportive of a relationship between life changes and a number of illness-related variables (e.g., physician visits, reports of physical health problems, reports of diagnosed illness, number of school days missed because of an illness), as assessed through subjects' self-reports.

Taken together, the research findings suggest a relationship between cumulative life changes and child health status. These findings are consistent with the adult literature that was briefly reviewed in Chapter 1. Unfortunately, due to the correlational nature of these investigations, the exact nature of the relationship between life change and child health status is unclear.

4

LIFE EVENTS AND PSYCHOLOGICAL ADJUSTMENT

Although many studies, like those considered in the previous chapter, have dealt with the relationship between life changes and physical health, child researchers have been equally concerned with the impact of life events on psychological and behavioral adjustment. This interest is not surprising given the widely held belief that stressors of various kinds can tax the adaptive capabilities of individuals to the point that they develop psychological difficulties and that developmental and other factors may render some children especially vulnerable to the effects of stress (Kagan, 1983).

Information regarding the association between life events and psychological adjustment comes primarily from two general types of investigations. The largest number consists of studies that have either compared children having "adjustment problems" of various types to some other group of children not thought to have adjustment problems (in terms of life events experienced) or that have focused on the relationship between life events and general measures of adjustment. A somewhat smaller number have dealt with the relationship between cumulative life change and specific forms of child psychopathology. In the following sections the nature of these studies are reviewed and the implications of their findings for a link between child/adolescent life stress and psychological difficulties are discussed.

LIFE STRESS AND GENERAL ADJUSTMENT

Group Comparison Studies

Two studies have focused on life event differences between children who display evidence of adjustment problems and those who do not.

One such study (Cowen, Weissberg, & Guare, 1984) was designed to assess those variables related to referral to a large ongoing school mental health project (Cowen et al., 1975). Teachers were asked to provide data regarding the occurrence, during the current school year, of major life changes experienced by 273 children referred for mental health services and 509 children who had not been referred. Information was obtained regarding 11 events that were seen as being relatively objective and observable (usually of an undesirable nature) and beyond the child's control. Examples included death or serious illness of a parent, sibling, or close relative; parents getting separated or divorced; and having a new adult or child move in with the family. General support for a relationship between life stress and mental health problems was provided by findings which suggested that referred children had experienced significantly higher levels of negative change during the school year. Specifically, a number of events (e.g., death in the family, serious illness in the family, separation/divorce, remarriage of a parent, family economic difficulties, new person in the home) occurred significantly more often in the case of children referred to the mental health program.

In a second study of this type, Sandler and Block (1979) obtained life stress measures on 99 kindergarten to third-grade children who were judged by their teachers to display emotional adjustment problems, as well as 44 children matched for grade, sex, and ethnic background who were not seen as displaying adjustment problems. Parents of both groups were asked to complete a behavior problem checklist as well as a life stress measure, adapted from the Coddington scale (which consisted only of items over which the child had no control). Several measures of life change were obtained, including a total life change unit score (Coddington, 1972a), a sum of the total number of events experienced, and indices of the number of desirable and of undesirable events experienced.

Several significant group differences were found. Maladjusted children, as a group, differed from controls in terms of the total number of events experienced, total life change unit scores, and the number of undesirable events experienced. No differences were found, however, when the measure of positive change was analyzed. Despite these overall differences, when the two groups were divided into children whose families were and were not on welfare, differences between groups held only for nonwelfare children.

Each of the life change scores, with the exception of the positive change index, was significantly related to maladjustment (as reflected in Behavior Problem Checklist scores), although these relationships held only for those children who had previously been judged by teachers to display psychological problems and whose families were not on welfare. These results suggest a relationship between life changes and behavioral maladjustment, but they also suggest that this relationship varies depending on the characteristics of the child and his or her social circumstances. The specific characteristics of welfare and nonwelfare children, which may mediate the impact of life stress, are unclear.

Additional information on the relationship between life stress and adjustment problems has also come from some of the health-oriented studies discussed in Chapter 3. For example, both Heisel et al. (1973) and Hodges et al. (1984) obtained scores on groups of children referred for mental health services in addition to assessing life changes experienced by children with specific physical health problems. Each of these studies yielded data suggesting that child psychiatric patients experienced higher levels of life stress prior to the onset of their difficulties than did children without a history of psychiatric problems.

Correlational Studies

Along with the group comparison studies discussed in the preceding section, a larger number of investigations have focused on the correlation between life events and measures thought to reflect psychiatric symptomatology or general level of psychological adjustment (Barrera, 1981; Compas, Slavin, Wagner, & Vannatta, 1985; Gersten, Langer, Eisenberg, & Orzeck, 1974; Gersten, Langer, Eisenberg, & Simcha-Fagan, 1977; Greenberg et al., 1983; Lawrence & Russ, 1985; Sandler & Block, 1979; Swearingen & Cohen, 1985b). Each of these studies provides useful information, and several are of special interest in that they not only provide data regarding the relationship between life stress and adjustment indices but also yield information concerning variables that may play a stress-buffering role.

In an early study of this type, Sandler (1980) used the data obtained from the Sandler and Block (1979) study described earlier to examine further the relationship between child life stress and behavior problems. The major purpose of this additional study, however, was to determine whether the previously found relationship between life events and behavior problems varied as a function of the level of support experienced within the family. For purposes of this study, social support was operationally defined as having an older sibling and a two-parent as opposed to a one-parent family. Indexing social support in this manner, Sandler found that the degree of relationship between life change and Behavior Problem Checklist scores did, in fact, depend on whether children displayed higher rather than lower levels of support (e.g., the relationship between life change and adjustment was stronger with lower levels of support than with higher levels of support). Although the index of social support used in this study might be faulted (as it does not adequately consider sources of support outside the family or the actual support provided by family members), the results of this study are relatively consistent with those that have been found in subsequent investigations employing more adequate measures.

In one of these studies, Barrera (1981) obtained measures of negative life change (using a select list of 27 events drawn from the Coddington scale) and adjustment from a sample of 86 pregnant adolescents from diverse ethnic backgrounds (mean age: 17 years). The adjustment measure selected for use in this study was the Brief Symptom Inventory (Derogatis, 1977), which yields measures of anxiety, depression, and somatization as well as a total symptom score. To test the hypothesis that the relationship between life events and adjustment would vary as a function of the adequacy of the subjects' social support network, an index of social support (the Arizona Social Support Interview Schedule [ASSIS]) developed by the author was also obtained on all subjects.

In terms of results, negative change was significantly related to measures of anxiety and depression as well as the total number of symptoms displayed. Of special interest was the finding that the relationship between negative change and depression varied as a function of the size of the individual's social support system. For example, the correlation between negative change and depression was found to be much smaller for those subjects with good social support networks ($r = 25$) than for those with less adequate support networks ($r = .60$). Although this study can be faulted for its reliance on a self-report methodology (and it is unclear why the link between events and other adjustment measures did not vary as a function of support), the results tentatively suggest that social support may play a stress-buffering role, protecting the individual from certain adverse effects of life change.

A study that is similar in many respects was conducted by Lawrence and Russ (1985). The subjects in this study were 66 sixth and seventh graders drawn from a parochial school. Measures obtained on each child included the Coddington life event scale, the Arizona Social Support Interview Schedule (ASSIS; Barrera, 1981), and the Brief Symptom Inventory (Derogatis, 1977). Also obtained were scores on the Harter (1982) Perceived Competence Scale for Children. This latter measure is a brief questionnaire designed to assess students' perceived competence in cognitive, social, physical, and general domains.

When only negative events from the Coddington Life Events Record were considered, a significant relationship between life change and overall symptoms was found. This relationship, however, was found to hold only for females. The correlation between stress scores and symptoms was .65 for females but only .14 for males, and the differences between these two correlations was statistically significant.

To test the hypothesis that the relationship between negative change and symptomatology would vary as a function of perceived competence and social support, additional multiple regression analyses were accomplished. These analyses suggested significant interactions between life stress and both of these variables in the prediction of total symptoms. Given a high level of life stress, those with low perceived competence and low levels of social support displayed the highest level of symptomatology. Additional analyses suggested that when these two variables were considered simultaneously (in interaction with life stress), support for their combined effects was also found. Thus the relationship between life stress and symptomatology was found to be weaker (perhaps suggesting that life stress has less effect on the person) when measures of personal competence *and* support were considered than when either variable was considered alone. Consistent with the sex differences reported earlier, the moderating effects of these variables were found to be stronger for females. These results are quite consistent with those of Barrera (1981) in providing support for the stress-buffering role of social support. Additionally, they provide tentative support for the moderating effects of perceived competence and suggest the importance of attending to sex difference in studies of child and adolescent life stress.

Finally, additional support for the importance of social relationships as a moderator of stress effects has been provided by Greenberg et al. (1983), who focused on the relationship between negative change and adjustment as reflected in measures of self-esteem and life satisfaction. In this study 213 junior and senior high students were administered the Life Events Checklist (Johnson & McCutcheon, 1980), the Tennessee Self Concept Scale (Fitts, 1965), and a brief rating scale designed to provide an index of life satisfaction. Subjects were also administered the Inventory of Adolescent Attachments, a measure developed by the author to assess the "affective quality (felt security) of the adolescent's relationship with their parents and peers" (Greenberg et al., 1983, p. 378).

Measures of negative life change were found to be significantly related to both dependent measures (positive change was also found to relate to self-esteem, although the degree of relationship was not as strong). Of special interest, however, was a significant interaction between negative change and parental attachment, suggesting that a positive high-quality affective relationship with one's parents may buffer the negative effects of stress on self-esteem. No support was found for the stress-buffering role of peer attachments.

Although several of the studies presented here seem to suggest that social support may play a significant role in minimizing the impact of stressful life changes, not all studies have yielded this type of finding. Compas et al. (1985), for example, in a study relating life changes to measures of adjustment (Hopkins Symptom Checklist), found negative changes to be significantly correlated with adjustment indices but that the stress-adjustment relationship did not vary as a function of support. Although its stress-buffering role was not documented (by finding an interaction between measures of life stress and support), social support was found to be directly related to adjustment measures (high levels being correlated with better adjustment). In this study the relationship between negative change and adjustment measures did vary as a function of subject sex; the correlation between negative change and adjustment was .49 (p < .001) for males but only .14 (n.s.) for females. These findings are consistent with Lawrence and Russ (1985) in emphasizing the need to consider sex differences, but they are at odds with respect to which sex displays the highest correlation between stress and adjustment measures. Clearly, further studies of the role of sex effects in life stress research are needed.

Although not addressing the issue of moderator variables, Gersten et al. (1974) have likewise provided data concerning life change and general psychological impairment, employing a large sample of 674 children and adolescents. In this study measures of life stress were obtained by questioning mothers of subjects about the occurrence of 25 life events during the previous five years. Mothers were also questioned to obtain information about psychological difficulties. Based on these interview data, indices of anxiety, self-destructive tendencies, conflict with parents, mentation problems, fighting, delinquency, and isolation were obtained, as was a total score and an index reflecting behavior change over the preceding five years.

Each of these measures was significantly correlated with total life change scores. When separate correlations between measures of positive and negative change and dependent measures were examined, however, the results suggested that primarily negative change was associated with psychological impairment, although anxiety was found to be correlated with both positive and negative change.

Despite the results presented to this point, not all life stress/adjustment studies have yielded totally positive findings. Indeed, some of the better-controlled studies in this area have provided data challenging the notion of a causal relationship between life stress and adjustment problems. One example is a study of Gersten et al. (1977). These investigators studied 1,034 children between the ages of 6 and 18 who were randomly selected from a cross-section of households in downtown Manhattan, New York. Mothers of these children were initially interviewed to obtain a measure of overall child psychological impairment, as well as indices of problems in the specific areas (e.g., parental conflict, anxiety, isolation, fighting, delinquency, mentation problems) assessed in the Gersten et al. (1974) study described above. Information was also obtained regarding a range of social and family variables that were thought to be reflective of "stressful processes" affecting the child and family. Included here was information regarding ethnic background, parental education, welfare status, number of children in the family, number of natural parents in the home, quality of the marital relationship, number of changes of residence, and mother's psychiatric symptomatology, among other variables. Approximately five years later, mothers of 732 of these children were interviewed again to determine which of 26 life events their children had experienced since the initial assessment and to again obtain data that would allow the investigators to derive adjustment measures such as those obtained during the first assessment.

The results suggested that measures of life change (particularly undesirable changes) were significantly correlated with the majority of adjustment measures regardless of whether these were obtained before or after the occurrence of life events. These findings cause one to question a causal relationship in which life stress results in problems of adjustment; with this type of relationship one would expect life stress scores to correlate most highly with subsequent (rather than prior) measures of adjustment. The fact that life stress was found to be as highly correlated with prior adjustment suggests the possibility that problems of adjustment result in increased levels of life change or that both result from some other factor. Additional multiple regression analyses further questioned the causal role of life stress in suggesting that despite the significant correlations between life stress and adjustment measures, negative life change was not found to be predictive of adjustment indices (obtained at Time 2) once initial level of adjustment (as assessed at Time 1) and social and family variables were statistically controlled. The authors concluded that life changes, in and of themselves, are unlikely to contribute measurably to problems of adjustment. Rather, they suggest that the commonly found relationships between life changes and adjustment actually result from the fact that both of these variables are the result of the child being exposed to what they refer to as "stressful processes" in the environment. From this point of view, being in a family that is poverty stricken, in which there is continuous marital discord, or in which a parent is continually displaying serious psychiatric problems is assumed to result in the experiencing of undesirable life changes within the family *and* to the development of childhood disturbance.

The failure to demonstrate that life stress is related to later adjustment once initial level of disturbance and social/family variables are partialed out of the equation is problematic for any assumption of causality. However, there are a variety of problems with this investigation that make it a relatively weak test of the etiological role of life events (Swearingen & Cohen, 1985b). For example, measures of life stress and measures of child adjustment were both provided by the mothers of subjects rather than by children themselves. This means that measures of child adjustment may have related more to maternal perceptions than to child adjustment per se. It is unclear, as well, whether events reported by the mothers were actually experienced as stressful by the child. Also, assessing life stress over a period of five years is problematic, as one might not expect events experienced as long as three to five years ago still to exert an impact on level of adjustment. Recall of events may also be impaired as the length of time assessed increases. A final issue is that the distinction made in this study between "stressful processes" and life events was not entirely clear. Measures of stressful social variables included such things as having parents who quarrel and who have an unhappy marriage, changing addresses frequently, having a mother with a psychiatric disorder, having "cold" parents, and having a parent on welfare. Among the life events assessed were "parents separated," "parents divorced," "family had to move," "mother in therapy," "mother institutionalized," and "unemployment status made it hard to feel warm and loving to the child." Given the very close association between what are considered by the authors to be "stressful processes" and stressful life events, it is not surprising that life events were unrelated to adjustment once the variance related to these social measures was partialed out. This failure to separate a "process" from life events represents a major limitation of the study (Swearingen & Cohen, 1985b).

Despite these limitations, this study suggests that any assumptions of causality in life stress research must be carefully considered. Indeed, as will be seen in Chapter 5, several more recent studies by Swearingen and Cohen (1985b), and by Compas and his colleagues (Compas & Wagner, 1985; Compas, Wagner, Slavin, & Vannatta, 1985) have also yielded data questioning the existence of a direct unidirectional causal relationship in which life stress results in problems of adjustment. Thus although several studies in this section appear to support a relationship between life events and adjustment measures, the nature of these relationships is unclear at this time. Similar statements might be made regarding studies to be presented in the following section that have focused on the relationship between life stress and more specific types of psychological and behavioral difficulties.

LIFE STRESS AND
SPECIFIC PROBLEMS OF ADJUSTMENT

Life Stress, School Adjustment, and School Performance

Sterling, Cowen, Weissberg, Lotyczewski, and Boike (1985) recently provided data regarding a possible relationship between life stress and school adjustment. Subjects for this study were drawn from a pool of 974 primary-grade children. In a manner similar to that used by Cowen et al. (1984) described earlier, each child's teacher was asked to provide information concerning whether the child had experienced any of 11 major negative life events during the school year. According to the teachers, 211 children experienced at least one major life event. The study itself involved comparing children who had experienced one or more major life changes to a control group of children who had not experienced major life changes and who were matched with the life stress group on relevant measures (e.g., age, sex, ethnic background, number of times retained in grade). Measures used to assess differences between these groups included the Classroom Adjustment Rating Scale (CARS; Lorion, Cowen, & Caldwell, 1975) and the Health Resources Inventory (HRI; Gersten, 1976). Briefly, the CARS includes 41 problem behaviors that are rated by teachers on a 5-point scale of severity. Scoring yields measures related to acting out in the classroom, showing shy/anxious behavior, and having difficulty learning along with a total score. The HRI is a 54-item measure composed of five factors (good student, adaptive assertiveness, peer sociability, follows rules, frustration tolerance) specifically assessing school-related competencies.

Support for a relationship between life stress and school problems is suggested by findings indicating that the two groups differed significantly on eight of the ten dependent variables considered (all but acting out [CARS] and follows rules [HRI]).

Additional analyses designed to assess the relationship between the amount of life stress experienced and school-related difficulties also yielded significant findings. Significant relationships were found between the number of events experienced (one, two, three, or more) and seven of the ten measures derived from the CARS and the HRI. Although there are serious limitations associated with assessing life stress via teacher report (teachers may not be aware of certain major life changes experienced by children), and with obtaining both life stress and school adjustment measures from the same source, these findings provide at least tentative support for a link between child life stress and school-related difficulties.

Fontana and Dovidio (1984) also provided data to suggest that increased levels of life change may have an adverse impact on an adolescent's performance in the school situation. In this study, 148 male and female senior high school students were administered the high school version of the Coddington Life Events Record (which retrospectively assessed life events occurring over the previous 12 months) and the student version of the Jenkins Activity Survey (Glass, 1977). Information regarding student's grade-point average over the past 12 months was obtained, as was information regarding involvement in extracurricular activities, days absent from school, and delinquent behaviors known to school administrators.

A unique feature of this investigation was the use of the modified Jenkins Activity Survey to study the potential stress-moderating role of Type A and Type B behavioral characteristics. The so-called Type A and Type B behavioral styles (Friedman & Rosenman, 1974) have been studied extensively in adults, particularly in regard to the relationship between these behavioral styles and the risk of coronary heart disease. Type A individuals (characterized by high levels of achievement motivation, an exaggerated sense of time urgency, aggressive tendencies, etc.), unlike Type B individuals (who show either an absence or less evidence of these features), have been shown to be at significantly greater risk for heart disease (Rosenman, Friedman, Straus, Jenkins, Zyzanski, & Messinger, 1970). Noting that research has also suggested that Type A and Type B individuals differ in their ability to cope with laboratory stressors, Fontana and Dovidio sought to assess the relationship between life stress and academic-related behaviors as a function of Type A-Type B status.

Results of this study suggested no overall differences between Type A and Type B students on any of the school-related measures. Additionally, no differences were found between Type A and Type B students in terms of the amount of life stress they had experienced during the previous 12 months. Significant overall relationships were found, however, between the total level of life stress experienced the previous year, grade-point average, and the degree of the student's involvement in sports. Higher levels of life stress were related to lower grades and involvement in fewer sports.

Analyses of the relationship between life stress and school performance, as a function of Type A-Type B status, provided tentative support for the view that adolescents with different response styles may be differentially affected by life stress. Significant (negative) relationships between life stress and indices of grade-point average and sports involvement (and a significant positive relationship between life stress and reported delinquent behavior) were found to hold only for Type B individuals. The only significant relationship found for Type A individuals was a correlation between increased levels of life change and number of school absences. Although events judged to be controllable and uncontrollable were assessed separately in these analyses, the general relationships between life changes and school performance that were found did not vary significantly as a function of the degree of control one could exert over those events experienced.

In general, the results of this study suggest that cumulative life changes are significantly related to decreased levels of academic performance in adolescents and that the effects of life stress on academic performance are most pronounced in adolescents with Type B behavioral characteristics. One might question the adequacy of a dependent measure consisting simply of reports of delinquent behaviors that are known to school authorities (as school personnel may be unaware of many delinquent activities); however, the results also suggested a relationship between life stress and conduct-disordered behaviors—a relationship that also varies as a function of Type A-Type B status. These latter findings, related to life stress and delinquency, are consistent with those obtained by Vaux and Ruggiero (1983), who documented a relationship between life change and self-reported delinquent behaviors in a large sample of 531 tenth and eleventh graders, and with findings by Bruns and Geist (1984) and Gad and Johnson (1980) that indicate increased levels of life change are significantly related to adolescents' self-reports of drug use.

Life Stress, Childhood Depression, and Suicidal Behavior

In addition to several studies cited earlier that have provided data on the relationship between life stress and depression, within the context of larger investigations (see Barrera, 1981; Cohen & Swearingen, 1985a; Johnson & McCutcheon, 1980), some investigators have focused specifically on childhood depression and have provided additional information on the link between stress and depressive features. Others have gone further in investigating the relationship between life stress and childhood suicide.

Friedrich, Reams, and Jacobs (1982), studying 132 white eighth and ninth graders (mean age: 14 years), obtained data on the amount of life stress experienced (Coddington scale) as well as measures of social support (Chan & Perry, 1981), the nature of the adolescent's family environment (Moos, 1974), and level of depression (as assessed by the

Beck Depression Inventory). Information concerning a number of demographic variables (e.g., parent's occupation, parent's educational level) was also collected. Multiple regression analyses employing combinations of psychosocial and demographic variables (e.g., life stress, family environment measures, social support) as predictors and depression scores as the dependent measure suggested that two variables were significantly related to adolescent depression. These included life stress scores and the Cohesion measure of the Family Environment Scale (assumed to assess concern and commitment to the family and to reflect family support). These two variables, taken together, were found to account for 71% of the total variance in Beck Depression Inventory scores. The importance of life stress in this relationship was suggested by the fact that cohesion scores accounted for only 16.7% of this variance after life stress scores were entered in the equation. When these two variables were considered in subsequent analyses, along with demographic variables found to be related to depression scores (e.g. maternal and paternal occupation, grades), life stress scores and family cohesion again emerged as the most powerful correlates of depression, along with one demographic index: parental occupation status. Life stress was again found to account for the largest proportion of the variance.

Information regarding the relationship between life stress and depression in younger children (134 fourth, fifth, and sixth graders) has been provided by Mullins, Siegel, and Hodges (1985). In this study the occurrence of life events (similar to those included in the Coddington scale) experienced during the previous 12 months was assessed by interviewing children individually—a procedure that may provide more adequate data than those usually obtained simply by having children fill out an events checklist on their own. In addition to deriving an overall stress score, by summing life change units associated with those events experienced, both positive and negative change scores were obtained by summing life change units of events judged to be positive and negative. Finally, positive and negative change scores were also derived by having the children themselves indicate whether the events they had experienced were positive or negative. The children also assigned positive and negative impact ratings to each event. Positive and negative scores were obtained by summing the impact ratings associated with each of the positive and each of the negative events experienced. In addition to obtaining life stress measures, the children were administered the Children's Depression Inventory (Kovacs, 1980), a 27-item multiple-choice measure that was developed to assess the motivational, cognitive, affective, and somatic symptoms of child depression.

Consistent with the previous findings, correlational analyses suggested a significant relationship between the measure of total life change (sum of life change units) and childhood depression. When separate analyses designed to look at the differential relationship between positive and negative change and depression scores were accomplished, the measure of negative (but not positive) change was found to be significantly related to Child Depression Inventory scores. Negative change scores, derived by summing life change unit values and by summing self-ratings of event impact, were found to be equally predictive of child-depression scores.

In a study related to the issue of depression, Cohen-Sandler, Berman, and King (1982) attempted to establish a connection between life stress and child and adolescent suicidal behavior. These investigators studied a total of 76 children between the ages of 5 and 14 years who were consecutively discharged from a medical center inpatient psychiatric unit. Based on information obtained during their hospitalization (e.g., family history, intake summary, presenting symptoms, behavior on the unit), children were assigned to one of three groups: (a) children who were suicidal, (b) those who were depressed but not suicidal, or (c) psychiatric control subjects (children who were hospitalized for psychiatric problems but who were considered neither depressed nor suicidal).

The children's medical records yielded information regarding life events experienced during the 12 months prior to admission, as well as data concerning life changes experienced during each of four specific periods of development: infancy (birth to 1 year, 5 months); preschool (1 year, 6 months to 4 years, 5 months); early childhood (4 years, 6 months to 8 years, 5 months); and later childhood/early adolescence (8 years, 6 months to 14 years, 11 months). Life stress scores for these four periods as well as for the 12 months prior to admission were derived by summing life change units (Coddington, 1972b) associated with each event experienced.

Suicidal children were found to have experienced significantly higher levels of stress during the 12 months prior to admission than either the depressed children or children displaying other types of psychiatric difficulties. When total level of life stress experienced over the life span was considered, suicidal children were also shown to have experienced significantly higher levels of overall life change. Specifically, these children were found to have experienced events more often such as birth of a sibling, separation and divorce of parents, remarriage of a parent, hospitalization of a parent, having a third adult become a part of the family (e.g. grandparent), death of a grandparent, and psychological trauma (e.g., observing the death of a grandparent or friend, witnessing the attempted murder of one parent by the other) than did children in the depressed and psychiatric control groups. When the level of life stress experienced by the three groups was considered across the four developmental periods (e.g., infancy, preschool, early childhood, later childhood), from preschool on the amount of life stress experienced increasingly differentiated suicidal children from children in the other groups; these differences reached statistical significance by the later childhood years. These differences are depicted in Figure 4.1. Although the fact that life stress scores were derived from children's medical records (which may not have contained information regarding many stressful events actually experienced) represents a limitation of the study, as does the retrospective attempt to assess life stress over such a long period of time, these findings are suggestive and in need of careful replication.

In considering the findings of this study, it is of interest to recall the case of Jason used to introduce Chapter 1. When Jason was about 2 years old, a younger sibling was born. Shortly after this, Jason's parents were separated and divorced, with the father getting custody of both children. When he was about 3 years old, his sister was diagnosed as having a chronic life-threatening illness that subsequently resulted in her having to be hospitalized on numerous occasions. At age 4 or 5 he and his sister were kidnapped by their natural mother. At around the age of 6 his father remarried and was divorced again within a period of eight months. Within the six months prior to Jason's referral to a mental health facility, he watched as a horse his uncle was trying to train fell on his uncle's head, which resulted in the uncle's eye being dislodged from its socket and subsequent blindness in both eyes. Finally, within three months of the referral, his uncle's wife (of whom Jason was very fond) unexpectedly committed suicide. Considering the findings of the research presented here, it is noteworthy that Jason experienced many of the events found to discriminate between suicidal and nonsuicidal patients (e.g., birth of a sibling,

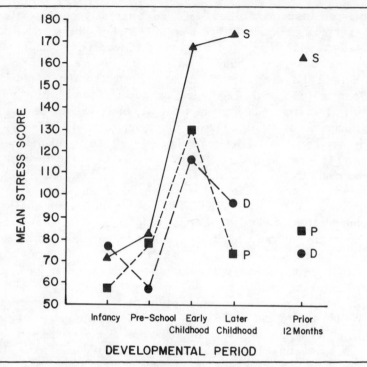

Figure 4.1   Mean stress scores across the lifespan: Suicidal (S) versus Depressed (D) and Psychiatric groups (P). Source: Cohen-Sandler, Berman, and King (1982). Reprinted by permission.

hospitalization of a family member, separation and divorce of parents, remarriage of parent, severe psychological trauma) and that he had experienced increasing levels of life stress as he became older as well as a cluster of significant events during the months preceding his referral. Of special note is the fact that Jason's father's concern over possible suicidal feelings precipitated the referral.

In general, the findings of a relationship between cumulative life change and suicidal tendencies presented here are consistent with those of Paykel (1974) showing that suicidal adults demonstrate higher levels of life stress than either depressed patients or normal controls. Again, additional work in this area is warranted.

Life Stress and Anorexia Nervosa

To some extent, findings related to life stress and anorexia nervosa might just as well have been presented in the preceding chapter on physical health problems, as this disorder is manifested in physical as well as psychological symptoms. This disorder, which often has its onset during adolescence, is characterized by severe (and often life-threatening) weight loss associated with an active refusal to eat, an intense fear of becoming obese, and a disturbance in body image—the person may claim to feel or be fat even while becoming more and more emaciated (American Psychiatric Association, 1980).

Among those with anorexia nervosa, at least two major subtypes have been distinguished. The most common distinction is between anorexics who attempt to lose weight simply through fasting and those whose fasting alternates with bulimia and subsequent vomiting or laxative use. In addition to displaying all the usual features of anorexia nervosa, this bulimic subgroup may show frequent episodes of uncontrolled binge eating, when they may consume extremely large quantities of high-caloric foods within a short period of time. They may see the binge eating as abnormal but be unable to control it, and may fear not being able to stop eating once they begin. In these cases there is usually an alternation of binge eating and the use of fasting, laxatives, and self-induced vomiting, all of which are designed to rid the body of the large amount of food eaten (Schwartz & Johnson, 1985). Studies of these subgroups are just beginning, but some evidence suggests that anorexics with bulimia differ from those without it in degree of psychopathology. Binge eaters/vomiters have been shown to display high levels of depression, and suicide has been reported to be the most common cause of death in this disorder (Maloney & Klykylo, 1983).

Although the etiology of anorexia nervosa is not known, it has often been assumed to be related to psychological factors and, for this reason, has frequently been considered as one example of a psychosomatic or psychophysiological disorder. Many writers have noted that the onset of the disorder is often preceded by a range of events such as death or serious illness in the family, personal illness, school failure, or major changes in relationships with others (Dally, 1969). Such comments have usually been based on casual observations, rather than on formal assessment of life stress; however, there have recently been attempts to investigate formally the relationship between cumulative life changes and anorexia nervosa.

In one recent investigation, Strober (1984) studied a total of 50 adolescents (mean age: 15½ years) with a diagnosis of anorexia nervosa who were consecutive admissions to the adolescent service of a large teaching hospital. Of these patients, 25 were designated as restricters (who sought to maintain weight loss through fasting) and 25 were anorexics who also displayed bulimic episodes. These two groups were matched on variables such as social class, age, duration of illness, percentage of weight loss, and so forth. Measures of life stress were obtained via a semistructured interview (focusing on events listed in the Coddington Life Events Record) conducted by a trained social worker who was unaware of the hypotheses of the study (e.g., that these groups would differ in terms of life stress and that they would show higher levels of stress than normals). Events experienced during each six months of the 18-month period preceding onset of the disorder were used to derive life stress scores.

Highly significant differences were found between bulimic and restricting anorexics when the amount of life stress experienced during the year and a half prior to symptom onset was considered. Bulimics experienced an average of 16.2 events, and restricters experienced a mean of only 7.8 events. Overall group differences were found for each of the three six-month periods considered in the study. There was evidence, however, to suggest that bulimic patients experienced rather constant levels of life stress but restricters showed increased levels during the most recent six months prior to onset. To compare the life stress scores of these two groups with those of normal adolescents of a similar age, life stress scores for the 12 months preceding onset of the disorder were computed so that these could be compared with the normative data for junior and senior high female adolescents provided by Coddington (1972b). Here mean life stress scores of 522 and 284 were found for bulimics and restricters, respectively, as compared with the normative group mean of 218. Life stress scores obtained by bulimic patients also correlated significantly with severity of bulimia (and level of depression), as rated by staff who were unaware of subjects' life stress scores. The findings obtained here suggest that although both groups of anorexics are characterized by higher levels of life stress than normals, cumulative life change is most highly related to bulimic symptoms in those with anorexia nervosa. The results are quite consistent with those obtained in an earlier study by the same investigator, which employed a smaller clinical sample (Strober, 1981); the study found life stress to differentiate between these same two types of anorexics.

SUMMARY

To the extent that the literature reviewed in Chapter 3 suggests a relationship between life stress and child health problems, the bulk of the studies reviewed in this chapter suggest that life changes are significantly related to child/adolescent adjustment. Several types of data provide support for this relationship. Studies have found life stress scores of children and adolescents to be significantly related to measures of anxiety and depression and to be correlated with decreased levels of self-esteem, an external locus of control orientation, delinquent behavior, poorer school performance, and overall level of psychiatric symptomatology. Some studies have also suggested that children and adolescents displaying specific types of psychological problems (e.g., suicidal tendencies, anorexia nervosa) show increased levels of life stress.

The issue of moderator variables will be considered in greater detail in Chapter 5, but it should be noted that several studies reviewed here assessed variables assumed to influence the child's response to stressful events (e.g., social support, parental attachment, Type A-Type B behavioral style). The resultant findings, indicating that life changes may relate to adjustment problems with some children but not others, strongly suggest the importance of considering such variables in child life stress research, rather than focusing on a direct linear relationship between life stress and adjustment-related outcomes.

Finally, although the literature reviewed here is for the most part supportive of some link between life stress and indices of psychological adjustment, many of the studies are plagued by methodological problems of one kind or another that make clear interpretation of the findings difficult. And some studies have questioned the existence of a causal relationship in which life stress contributes to problems of child adjustment. In Chapter 5 the nature of the methodological issues that arise when conducting life stress research will be discussed in greater detail so that the findings presented in this and the previous chapter can be placed in proper perspective.

5

CONCEPTUAL AND METHODOLOGICAL ISSUES IN CHILD LIFE STRESS RESEARCH

The preceding chapters explored a range of studies that have found significant links between measures of child/adolescent life events and indices of physical health and psychological adjustment. Although these findings are *consistent* with the view that life stress plays a significant role in the development and/or maintenance of health and adjustment problems, methodological limitations inherent in many studies make it difficult to draw firm conclusions regarding the impact of life changes on individuals or the nature of those relationships that have been documented. This chapter deals with a range of conceptual and methodological issues that must be considered when interpreting the results of these child stress studies and conducting research in the area.

ON THE MAGNITUDE OF LIFE STRESS-HEALTH/ADJUSTMENT RELATIONSHIPS

Although significant correlates of life stress have been found in numerous studies, it is instructive to examine the magnitude of the correlations obtained. Correlations in the .30 to .40 range are most often reported. Although correlations of this magnitude are often statistically significant with reasonably large Ns, they suggest that life change accounts for a relatively small proportion of the variance in the dependent measures employed. This rather sobering fact suggests that our ability to make accurate predictions based on life stress scores alone is much less than would be desirable. Thus even if one can assume that there is a causal relationship of the type where life stress causes health/adjustment problems (more will be said later about the likelihood of this), the direct impact of life stress on health and adjustment is not great when the child/adolescent population as a whole is considered.

The reason for this state of affairs is unclear, but several factors may be involved. One factor may relate to the nature of life stress measures that have been used in previous studies. Several approaches to the assessment of life change have been used and these measures vary in terms of demonstrated validity and reliability. Thus the low correlations obtained may be due in part to inadequate methods of measurement and therefore may not reflect the actual magnitude of stress-dependent measure relationships. Life stress measures have also varied in the degree to which they have focused on the assessment of life change per se as opposed to providing for the separate assessment of desirable and undesirable change. Measures have also differed in the ways the stressfulness or impact of life events has been indexed. As we will see later (and as was discussed in Chapter 2), some of these measures typically yield higher correlations with indices of health and adjustment than do others. However, even these higher correlations are usually of only moderate magnitude. This suggests that factors other than measurement variables contribute to the low correlations that have typically been obtained.

A second possible contributor to the low correlations may have to do with the fact that individuals experience stessors other than those usually reflected in life change measures. For example, with one notable exception (see Compas et al., 1985), child and adolescent life change measures fail to assess many frequently occurring day-to-day stressors such as peer pressure, negative interactions with teachers, conflict with parents, and the like. To the extent that these daily hassles (Kanner et al., 1981; Lazarus, DeLongis, Folkman, & Gruen, 1985) result in stress that is not assessed by life change measures, one might assume that correlations between life change measures and measures of health and adjustment will be attenuated. Indeed, studies by Lazarus and his colleagues (see DeLongis et al., 1982; Kenner et al., 1981; Lazarus et al., 1985) conducted with adults have suggested that measures of daily hassles may be more highly correlated with health-related measures than are measures of major life changes. Some of the strongest correlations reported with adolescent subjects have been found by Compas et al. (1985), who used a measure that assesses both

major life changes and daily stressors. Again, the low-magnitude correlations often reported may be related in part to the failure of life
change measures to assess relevant microstressors in addition to major
life events. In addition to these stressors, there are likely to be others
of a more chronic nature (e.g., having a physical handicap; knowing
that one is likely to develop some sort of serious illness) that, if not
assessed, will serve to reduce life stress-health/adjustment correlations. In this regard it is important to underline the fact that major life
changes represent only one class of potential stressors to which the
person may be exposed. If stressors of various types bear some relationship to child health and adjustment—and we assess only some of
these (in the form of major life changes)—we cannot expect to find
really strong replicable relationships.

A third factor contributing to the low correlations between life
changes and dependent variables may be the failure of investigators to
consider variables that may moderate the effects of life change. The
role of moderator variables will be considered in more detail later, but
it can be noted here that individuals display marked variability in their
response to potential stressors. Some seem to withstand the effects of
adversity well; others develop significant difficulties when confronted
with what would objectively appear to be only moderately stressful
circumstances. Work with adults (and less frequently with children)
suggests that there are a variety of social and individual difference
variables that influence the person's response to life changes. To the
extent that these variables are not considered, only low to moderate
correlations can be expected. Despite the significant correlations reported, we know relatively little concerning the actual degree to which
life changes impact on the health and adjustment of children and
adolescents.

ISSUES IN CHILD/ADOLESCENT
LIFE STRESS ASSESSMENT

As indicated in the preceding section, there are a variety of assess-
ment-related issues that have implications for how research findings in
this area are to be interpreted. In addition to questions related to the
adequacy of individual life change measures (considered in Chapter

2), there are other questions regarding how life stress can best be conceptualized, the best method of quantifying the impact of life changes,
who should provide measures of life stress, and so on. Several of these
issues have been alluded to in the earlier discussion of assessment
measures. Each of them will now be addressed in more detail to see
what conclusions can be drawn from the existing literature.

Conceptualizing Life Stress:
Change versus Undesirability

As was indicated in Chapter 2, two basic types of measures have
been used in most child life stress research. Measures such as the Coddington Life Events Record are based on the assumptions that all life
changes, positive *and* negative, require social readjustment, are
stressful, and can have a similar adverse impact on the individual.
Consistent with these assumptions, these measures have been constructed to yield only a single index of life stress. (The Family Inventory of Life Events and Changes [Patterson & McCubbin, 1983] is
similar in this respect.) In contrast, the development of measures such
as the Life Events Checklist, the Junior High Life Experiences Survey,
and the Adolescent Perceived Events Scale have been based on the
assumption that undesirable events may have a different and perhaps
more detrimental impact on the individual (than positive change), and
that life stress can best be conceptualized in terms of events that exert
a negative impact on the individual. As a result, these measures provide for the separate assessment of desirable and undesirable change.
Considering the research conducted to this point, what can be concluded regarding the merits of these two differing points of view?

As was noted in Chapter 1, a number of adult life stress studies
have addressed the change versus undesirability issue. For example, in
one early study, Vinokur and Selzer (1975) employed a modified version of the Schedule of Recent Experiences, designed to yield separate
measures of desirable and undesirable events in order to examine the
relationships between positive and negative change and adjustment.
Adjustment measures included self-ratings of depression, anxiety, and
tension, as well as indices of aggression, paranoia, and suicidal pro-
clivity. Significant correlations between life changes and the majority
of these variables were found when the index of negative change was

considered. Positive change was essentially uncorrelated with these measures. Mueller, Edwards, and Yarvis (1977) also examined the relationship between desirable and undesirable change and measures of psychiatric symptomatology. Like Vinokur and Selzer, they found that negative but not positive changes correlated with severity of symptoms. Further, an index of negative change was found to be more highly correlated with symptoms than was an overall life change index (derived by summing both desirable and undesirable life changes). Similarly, other studies with adults (Grant, Sweetwood, Yager, & Gerst, 1981; Ross & Mirowski, 1979; Sarason et al., 1978) also found measures of negative change to be more consistently and more highly related to psychological adjustment than scores based on reports of positive change. (For a review of adult studies related to this issue, see Thoits, 1983.)

Consistent with these findings, the results of several child/adolescent studies discussed in previous chapters also support the view that negative life changes are most highly correlated with adjustment indices. Several studies (Compas et al., 1985; Gad & Johnson, 1980; Gersten et al., 1974; Johnson & McCutcheon, 1980; Swearingen & Cohen, 1985a) have found measures of negative change to be more highly correlated with dependent measures than those of positive change (see also Newcomb, Huba, & Bentler, 1981). In those instances where positive change has been found to be significantly related to some dependent variable, the relationship has typically been in the opposite direction from that found with negative change. Positive change, for example, has been found to be related to *lower* rather than higher levels of depression (Swearingen & Cohen, 1985a) and *lower* rather than higher levels of maladjustment (Johnson & McCutcheon, 1980).

The majority of studies related to this issue have focused on the relationship between desirable and undesirable changes and indices of psychological adjustment. Less information is available regarding the relationship between positive and negative life changes and physical health outcomes, although three studies that considered health-related variables (Brand et al., 1986; Greene et al., 1985; Smith et al., 1983) all found negative changes to be more highly correlated with dependent measures than indices of positive change.

More work in this area is needed (especially related to physical health), but it seems that for the most part, it is undesirable change that has an adverse impact on health and adjustment (if indeed a causal relationship can be assumed). These results argue strongly for the separate assessment of positive and negative life changes and suggest that studies that do not assess desirable and undesirable events separately are likely to yield lower estimates of the relationship between life stress and dependent measures.

Assessing the Desirability/Undesirability Dimension

Assuming that it is important for life stress measures to provide separate indices of positive and negative change, how should this be accomplished? Should one attempt to develop separate lists of desirable and undesirable events, with the categorization of events being determined by agreement among independent raters? Or is it more appropriate to have subjects provide self-ratings of event desirability? Actually, the available research suggests either approach may be appropriate. For example, in studies by Vinokur and Selzer (1975) and Mueller et al. (1977), measures of desirable and undesirable change have been derived in both ways (e.g., by summing events rated as positive and as negative by subjects themselves, and by summing events rated as positive and negative by independent judges). Positive and negative life change scores obtained in each of these ways were found to be equally predictive of adjustment measures. These findings are from studies with adults, but similar findings have also been reported by Swearingen and Cohen (1985a) using an adolescent sample.

Despite the fact that these methods appear to yield somewhat similar findings, a case can be made for using a self-rating procedure with adolescents and children who are old enough to make these types of ratings. The major reason is that, as was discussed earlier, children as well as adults are quite variable in their views of events. Changing to a new school, for example, may be a very positive event for one child and a negative event for another. Likewise, children's perceptions of events such as "getting a new brother or sister," "parent getting a new job," "getting a new stepmother or stepfather," and so forth may be different depending on the circumstances surrounding the event and how these circumstances influence the way in which the event is appraised by the child. Although relying on a self-rating approach is clearly more subjective than using judges' ratings to derive measures of positive and negative change, this approach has the advantage of reflecting the desirability of events *as experienced by the in-*

dividual. As such, self-ratings would seem to have the potential for providing a more personalized and therefore more sensitive measure of event desirability. This is suggested by the fact that when judges' ratings are used to determine the desirability of events, the majority of the events are rated as ambiguous. Mueller et al. (1977), for example, had three independent judges rate some 40 events as to their desirability/undesirability. Eighteen of these events were considered to be ambiguous because of a lack of agreement among judges as to whether the events were generally positive or negative. A self-rating procedure is likely to provide for the assessment of a broader range of events, especially those that are most likely to be viewed differently by individuals. Although it may be preferable that life change measures allow for self-ratings of the desirability of events in those instances in which the child is old enough to provide such ratings, this may not be possible with younger children. In such cases it may be necessary for the parent rather than the child to provide information regarding life events experienced by the child and to use judges' ratings in determining events to be considered positive or negative.

Quantifying the Impact of Life Changes

The developers of child and adolescent life stress measures (like the developers of adult life change measures) have taken several approaches in attempting to quantify the impact of life changes. The most common approach has been to use life change units to index event impact (Coddington, 1972a; Holmes & Rahe, 1967). These units are purported to reflect the average amount of social readjustment resulting from a given event and are viewed as a general index of event stressfulness. Typically, a sum of the life change units associated with the experienced events is taken as an index of life stress. As was suggested earlier (Chapter 2), the fact that children vary in their appraisal of events, and in terms of whether specific events are seen as positive or negative, make it unlikely that life change unit scores will provide an adequate index of the actual impact of specific event on a given child. For example, the event "marriage of parent to stepparent" may be viewed as very positive by a child in elementary school who has a good relationship with the stepparent and who likes having this new person in the same house. Conversely, the event may be seen as very negative by another child, who neither gets along with nor likes the person his or her parent has married. It is unlikely that the life change unit of 65 (Coddington, 1972a) adequately reflects the degree of stressfulness experienced by both of these children as a result of this event. Because of this, some researchers in this area have advocated the use of individualized impact ratings to index the effects of life change. With the Life Events Checklist, for example, children are asked not only to list events they have experienced and to rate these as positive or negative but also to indicate the effect the event had on them along a 4-point scale (0 = no effect to 3 = great effect). Here the impact ratings of events rated as desirable and undesirable are summed in order to derive positive and negative change scores. Which of these approaches is preferable?

Each of the approaches has limitations. To date, a number of life stress studies conducted with both children and adults have considered optimal methods for weighting life changes. In terms of adult studies, Vinokur and Selzer (1975) found that correlations between unit scores (each event weighted 1), scores based on the self-rating of events, and life change unit scores were greater than .90; unit scores were as highly correlated with relevant dependent measures as were scores based on weighted events. Other adult studies (see Johnson & Sarason, 1979a; Ross & Mirowski, 1979) have provided similar findings. (For a review of these findings see Thoits, 1983.) In terms of child/adolescent studies, research with the Life Events Checklist has suggested that positive and negative change scores obtained by summing impact ratings are no more predictive of indices of health and adjustment than a sum of the number of positive and negative events experienced (with desirable and undesirable events being counted separately). Likewise, Newcomb et al. (1981) provided data on adolescents suggesting that the differential weighting of events provides no additional advantage over simple unit weights. Finally, data provided in the previously cited study by Swearingen and Cohen (1985) also suggest that a simple count of positive and negative events provides as good an index of life change as do measures derived by summing weighted events, no matter how they are weighted.

Although these findings suggest that the weighting of life events may be of little consequence, regardless of the method used, intuitively it seems likely that some events (divorce or death of a family member, for example) have a much greater impact on the child than other events (e.g., moving to a new home), and should thus be given a greater weighting. As Rahe (1974) suggested, the method of weighting may make little difference in group studies with individuals who experience moderate to low levels of life change and who, as a group, have not experienced increased levels of major life changes. He does suggest, however, that the differential weighting of events may be of greater value in quantifying life changes in individuals who have experienced high levels of life changes of a major type. This view may be supported by future studies, but the available findings suggest that a simple count of events may provide the most objective and efficient index of life change. However, although the usefulness of impact ratings and life change unit approaches to weighting events has not been confirmed, the separate assessment of positive and negative change has received strong and consistent support.

Distinguishing Between Categories of Life Change

Most life change measures simply provide respondents with lists of life events to which they respond by indicating those events experienced within some specified time period. These measures are usually scored without regard to the area(s) of one's life to which these events may have related. Possibly, the impact of certain types of events differs from one person to another. Some support for this notion comes from findings such as those provided by Felner, Stolberg, and Cowen (1975), which indicate that even events that are in some ways similar (in the sense that both involve loss of a parent), such as parental death and divorce, may have quite different outcomes; children of divorce tend to show more aggressive and antisocial behavior and children who have lost a parent through death tend to show problems of shyness and withdrawal. Based on findings such as these, Rutter (1983) suggested that events that involve loss or disappointment should be assessed separately from those having to do with disturbed interpersonal relationships, and that both of these types of events should be considered apart from other types of life changes. There are, in fact, relatively few data having to do with the relationship between different types of life events and measures of health and adjustment. The information that is available comes primarily from an investigation by Newcomb et al. (1981).

In this study the investigators used a specially constructed 39-item life change measure to study the relationship between life change and several indices of health and psychological functioning that were described as reflecting headache proneness, insomnia, injury hysteria, depression, trust in physicians, trust in medicine, illness sensitivity, and thought disorganization. Although the primary foci of the study dealt with a number of the issues discussed earlier (e.g., importance of event desirability, the optimal method for weighting events), an attempt was also made to determine relevant clusters of life events and the differential relationship between specific types of events and the dependent measures.

In order to determine whether meaningful clusters of life events could be defined, responses of 1,018 adolescents (grades seven through nine) to the life events measure were subjected to factor analysis. This analysis yielded seven interpretable factors, composed of three to eight events each, that accounted for 44% of the variance among the 39 items. These seven clusters included groups of items related to (a) family and parents (e.g., parents divorced); (b) accident/illness (e.g., death in the family); (c) sexuality (e.g., broke up with boyfriend or girlfriend; lost virginity); (d) autonomy (e.g, started driving; found new group of friends); (e) deviance (e.g., got in trouble at school); (f) relocation (e.g., family moved); and (g) distress (e.g., ran away from home). Only three of the 39 life events assessed did not load on any of these factors. The fact that interpretable factors could be defined through such analyses suggests that life events do not occur at random and that the occurrence of events in one area is likely to be associated with the occurrence of other events in the same area.

These investigators have also provided data tentatively suggesting that different types of events may be differentially related to dependent measures. This can best be illustrated by considering findings related to two of the eight dependent measures. When the index of headache proneness was considered, this variable was found to be significantly correlated with negative events in the family/parents, accident/illness, and distress categories only. No relationships between headache proneness and events in the sexuality, autonomy, deviance, or relocation categories were found. When the index of depression was considered, however, it was found to be correlated with all life event categories except those related to accidents/illness and autonomy.

Somewhat similar findings have also been provided by Compas et al. (1985). These investigators have assessed the relationship between these same seven life event clusters and measures of adjustment provided by the Hopkins Symptom Checklist. When negative life changes were studied in relation to the total symptom score, significant relationships were restricted to life events occurring in the family/parent, deviance, and distress areas. No significant relationships were found between symptoms and events in the accidents/illness, sexuality, autonomy, and relocation areas.

Life event measures have not generally provided for the separate assessment of different types of life events, but the preliminary findings presented here suggest that different types of events may lead to different outcomes and that the distinction between types of life events should be considered more often in the assessment of life changes.

The Time Period for Life Event Assessment

An important issue that has received relatively little attention in the literature is the period during which life changes should be assessed. For example, in studying the relationship between life change and health and adjustment, should we ask respondents to report events experienced during the past three months, the past six months, the past year, or the past ten years? Related to this question, existing child and adolescent measures are designed to assess events occurring over different periods. Usually the period assessed ranges from three months to one year, although investigators have frequently taken the liberty of modifying instructions to obtain reports over much longer periods. At present, there are few guidelines for making decisions regarding this issue. Two issues, however, deserve consideration in attempting to arrive at a best choice. One of these has to do with the reliability of event recall over time, the other with the temporal relationship between event occurrence and the development of health or adjustment problems.

Concerning the first issue, when using self-report life event questionnaires, the individual's ability to report events accurately may decrease with time. The extent of decrease seems to depend, at least in part, on the length of the interval over which events are assessed and the approach taken to assessment. To illustrate, one study with adults (Jenkins, Hurst, & Rose, 1979) asked subjects to self-report on life changes experienced during the preceding six months. Nine months later they were asked to report again on events occurring during that same period of time. The results suggested that depending on how events were weighted, stress scores obtained at the second testing were reduced between 34% and 46%. These findings caused the authors to question the validity of any retrospective report that included events occurring more than six months in the past. Other studies have also suggested declining reliability of event reporting with the passage of time.

Uhlenhuth, Shelby, Haberman, Balter, and Lipman (1977), for example, provided data suggesting that reports of life events decline with the passage of time, decreasing at a rate of about 5% per month over a 1½-year period. Decreased reporting of important events that were beyond the person's control occurred at an even faster rate. As Thoits (1983) noted, however, several other studies have suggested adequate reliability of recall over periods as long as one year. In attempting to account for the discrepancy in findings, those studies showing the best reliability of recall over time involved obtaining reports of life change via interviews, as opposed to the use of self-report life event measures. Given that interviews provide an opportunity to clarify responses and to probe for events that may have been forgotten and thus not reported spontaneously, this approach may have significant advantages in eliciting more reliable reporting over a longer period. When it is considered that these findings of declining recall over time have been obtained with adult subjects, and that the issue may be even more of a problem with children, assessing child life events over long time periods (e.g., more than six months) may be a risky venture. Although life event interviews have seldom been employed in obtaining child/adolescent life stress measures, such an approach might well be considered in those instances in which assessment over a longer period is desirable.

An additional issue to be considered in determining the period during which events are to be assessed relates to the presumed time lag between the experiencing of life events and symptom development. As Thoits (1983) noted, little is known regarding the temporal relationship between the occurrence of life events (or clusters of events) and the development of difficulties, or the amount of time necessary for these problems to be resolved. This lack of information makes it difficult to determine the optimal time period for life event assessment.

If psychological measures are taken too soon or too late after event impacts have occurred, no relationship or a very modest relationship between events and symptoms will be found. The low correlations between events and disturbance reported in most studies may be due, in fact, to these timing problems. Typically, studies correlate the number of events over, say, the past year with subject's current level of symptomatology or with some indicator of the presumed presence or absence of disturbance (e.g., patient versus nonpatient status). The lag between events and subsequent measurement of disturbance could be considerable. . . . thus, many life event studies may be underestimating the impact of life events on disturbance—enough time may have passed for symptom abatement to occur. (Thoits, 1983, pp. 46-47)

If little is known regarding this issue with adults, the situation is even more problematic with children and adolescents because there are few guidelines for choosing an optimal time period for assessment with this age group. Although more research is needed on this point, studies with children have assessed life stress over periods ranging from three months to several years. All the data are not in, but some of the strongest correlations reported have come from studies that have assessed events over relatively short periods (e.g., three months or so—see Compas et al., 1985). Unfortunately, it is not clear if these stronger correlations obtained are simply due to the greater reliability of measures over this shorter period of time, to the fact that these measures are superior to those used in other studies, or whether the findings are due to a more adequate timing of event assessment. Nevertheless, for reasons of both reliability and timing, it would be prudent to assess events over a shorter rather than a longer period. It is also essential that studies begin to address the issue of the temporal link between stressful life changes and health-related outcomes with children and adolescents.

The Source of Life Event Data:
Parent or Child as Respondent

In some instances questions arise concerning who should provide information on life events experienced by the child. In many ways it would seem obvious that such data are best provided by the child, especially if one wishes to take into account the child's appraisal of events and their impact on the child himself or herself. There are instances, however, when the child may be considered too young to provide an adequate recall of events experienced over a given period of time and the parent is seen as an acceptable source of information. Or a child might be unavailable, making it necessary to obtain data from a significant other. And there may be some instances, with particular types of studies, when it is thought that a parent may be able to provide less biased data than might be provided by the child. In reviewing the child/adolescent literature it is possible to find studies that have used both the child and the parent as a data source. Unfortunately, relatively little research is available to guide one in making decisions about this issue. Some preliminary findings, however, have been provided by Gilbert (1985).

In Gilbert's study 45 children and adolescents, ranging in age from 11 to 19 years, were administered the Johnson and McCutcheon (1980) Life Events Checklist. These subjects reported life events experienced during the previous year, rated these events as desirable or undesirable, and provided ratings regarding the impact each event had on their lives. From this information it was possible to derive positive and negative scores based on a simple count of events and by summing impact ratings of events rated as positive or negative. Parents of children and adolescents in the sample were also asked to respond to the Life Events Checklist for their children, and the same life stress scores were derived from these parent-completed measures.

Results of this study suggested only moderate correlations between life stress scores provided by parent and child. In terms of unit ratings (each event weighted 1), correlations between parent and child measures were .40 for a total number of positive events and .54 for total number of negative events. When positive and negative change scores were derived by summing impact ratings provided by parent and child, correlations of .48 and .60 were obtained for desirable and undesirable events, respectively. When the total number of events endorsed was considered, the correlation between parent and child scores was .35. This correlation was .50 when a sum of the impact ratings for all events experienced (positive and negative) was considered. Paired t-tests revealed significant differences between parents and children on all life stress measures, with children and adolescents reporting more events and having higher weighted scores.

Although these findings do not provide information concerning whether parents or children give the most accurate report of the events that were actually experienced, they do suggest that the measures obtained from these two sources are not identical and that parents may underreport or children and adolescents may overreport life events. Either of these possibilities has important implications for the nature and magnitude of the correlations found with dependent measures. This study simply provides information concerning the overall correlation between parent and child measures. It does not provide any index of the degree of agreement concerning the occurrence-nonoccurrence of specific events. Further studies that seek to determine the degree to which parents and children agree in their reports of specific events seem necessary to determine the specific types of events that are most frequently related to disagreement, and to assess other factors that may relate to differences in reporting. Although there are likely to be instances in which it is possible to obtain data from only one source, be that parent or child, in those instances where there is access to both it seems prudent to supplement child/adolescent data with information provided by parents whenever possible. Given disagreements, these may be best resolved through·the use of interview procedures, rather than relying solely on the use of life stress checklists.

ASSESSING STRESS-RELATED VARIABLES

Although it is essential that assessment issues such as those just discussed be taken into account in interpreting research findings and in planning research, the assessment of other variables is of no less importance. If a research study is to provide meaningful information on the relationship between life stress and problems of health and adjustment, one must not only adequately assess relevant life changes but also assess health/adjustment variables in a meaningful way and with valid measures. Many child/adolescent studies published to date have been deficient in this regard.

The need for more adequate assessment of dependent variables is especially relevant in considering studies related to life change and adjustment. An overview of studies presented in Chapter 4 suggests that the majority of these investigations have relied heavily on the use of self-report (or parent-report) measures of adjustment and on the use of single rather than multiple measures.

Some investigators have relied on measures designed to assess specific psychological variables. Examples include measures such as the Children's State-Trait Anxiety Inventory, the Child Depression Inventory, the Piers-Harris Self-Concept Scale, the Tennessee Self-Concept Scale, and the Rotter Locus of Control Scale. Other researchers have tended to rely more on psychiatric symptom checklists or on global measures of psychological maladjustment. Still others have relied on self-reports of behaviors, such as drug usage or delinquent acts, or on self-ratings of variables, such as the ability to cope with personal problems or the number of visits to the school counselor during the previous year. Although some of these measures have been reasonably well researched with child populations and are supported by at least some validity data (e.g., Child State-Trait Anxiety Inventory; Child Depression Inventory; Piers-Harris Self-Concept Scale), other measures have been developed primarily for use with adults, and their validity and reliability when used with children is largely unknown. And simple self-ratings of individual variables (e.g., ability to cope) are especially suspect. Thus although a variety of adjustment-related correlates of child life stress have been reported in the literature, the meaningfulness of these findings varies with the validity and reliability of the dependent measures employed.

Other studies, rather than attempting to correlate life stress with adjustment indices, have sought to assess differences in levels of life change between children with psychological problems and controls. For the most part, clinic groups have been selected for investigation based on rather subjective criteria (e.g., child being referred for mental health problems, teacher nomination of child as displaying adjustment problems). Because children may be referred to mental health facilities for a variety of reasons that are imperfectly correlated with actual child disturbance, studies comparing broad groups of "clinical cases" to "normal controls" can yield findings of only the most general type. Investigations designed to assess life stress characteristics of children who display well-documented psychological difficulties of a more specific nature are likely to yield more useful data.

Studies of life stress and physical health have also been plagued by problems in the assessment of health-related variables, although to a lesser degree. Although some studies in this area have relied on self-ratings of physical health status or self-reports of other variables (e.g., number of school days missed because of illness; diagnosed illnesses during past year), other studies have focused on more objective indices of illness. For example, Chapter 3 cited studies that utilized objective clinical indices of streptococcal infection, respiratory illness, diabetic control, and independent reports of illness episodes displayed by children with chronic illness. Also, those studies that have sought to assess differences in life stress between clinic and nonclinic groups have generally employed more well-defined groups of subjects than have investigators studying life stress-adjustment relationships.

Despite such problems sufficient studies have employed reasonably adequate measures to conclude that there is at least a general relationship between life changes and problems of child health and adjustment. Issues such as those considered here, however, limit our ability to draw firm conclusions regarding those specific problems that are most consistently related to the experiencing of stressful life changes and the magnitude of the relationship between life stress and health/adjustment problems.

CORRELATES OF LIFE STRESS:
PROBLEMS OF INTERPRETATION

Given research findings suggesting significant relationships between measures of life stress and problems of health and adjustment, are we to conclude that life stress contributes to the development of these difficulties? Unfortunately, a number of factors make it difficult to infer a causal relationship of this type. In order to make causal statements, it is usually considered necessary to conduct experiments in which some variable of interest is systematically manipulated and the effects of this manipulation on behavior observed. For both practical and ethical reasons, it is impossible to manipulate life stress as one might a laboratory stressor. Because of this problem, studies relating life stress to indices of health and adjustment have necessarily been correlational in nature. Although the results of such studies are of interest, one often cannot say whether life stress results in problems of health and adjustment, for example, or whether persons with such problems are simply more prone to experience life changes. It is also difficult to rule out the existence of other variables that may result both in high levels of life change and in health and adjustment problems. Clearly, the old caveat "correlation does not imply causation" is worth remembering when considering research findings in this area. In the following sections a range of factors that pose difficulties in making causal assumptions concerning the role of life events will be considered.

The Problem of Confounded Measurement

One factor that makes it difficult to assume a causal relationship has to do with the possible confounding of independent and dependent measures that is found in most studies. Difficulties in interpretation arise because many items contained in existing life stress scales may themselves be seen as manifestations of illness or problems of adjustment. Indeed, Hudgens (1974) suggested that as many as 29 of the 42 items making up the Holmes and Rahe (1967) adult measure fall into this category. Examples include items such as "sexual difficulties" and "trouble with boss." Items of this type found in child life stress measures would include events such as "suspension from school," "increased arguments with parents," "breaking up with boyfriend/girlfriend," "trouble with the police," and "failure in school." Although these events may, in reality, be quite stressful when experienced, the inclusion of these types of items in life stress measures has the potential of resulting in spuriously high correlations because of the confounding of independent (life stress) and dependent (health/adjustment) measures.

To what extent does such confounding account for the significant correlations reported in the life stress literature? A partial answer can be found in the results of several investigations designed to determine the correlations between dependent measures and two types of event scores—namely, scores based on events over which the subject has no control (and that could not be realistically viewed as consequences of problems), and scores based on events over which subjects have some degree of control. In one adult study, Mueller et al. (1977) found that although correlations were somewhat smaller, significant correlations between life stress and indices of adjustment were still found even when only events outside of the subject's control were assessed. With children, Sandler and Block (1979) employed a life stress measure consisting only of items outside the subject's control and found a significant relationship between life stress and behavior problem checklist scores. Although correlations were smaller than those found in an earlier study that included both types of events in the life stress measure, Gersten et al. (1977) found significant correlations between life stress and indices of adjustment when only events judged to be outside the subject's control were considered. In general, these results seem to suggest that the significant correlations between major life events and dependent measures reported in the literature are not simply the result of a confounding of measures.

Given that even those life events that are under the person's control may be stressful when experienced, life stress measures should include both types of events if the intent is to sample the domain of major stressful life changes. As Dohrenwend and Dohrenwend (1974) suggested, measures including both types of events may have a distinct advantage when the major purpose of the investigator is simply to predict the onset of difficulties. The two types of events, however, should be considered separately when conducting etiological research and in cases in which a confounding of events and "symptoms" may pose significant interpretive problems. Unfortunately, only a handful of the studies reported in previous chapters have limited the events assessed to those outside of the child's control. Although this does not mean that the correlations obtained are totally artifactual, it suggests that the magnitude of these correlations may be inflated to some unknown degree (Thoits, 1983).

The problem of confounded measures is an important issue in studies assessing major life changes and is perhaps of even greater concern in studies that assess more frequently occurring daily stressors. As was briefly noted in Chapter 2, a number of investigators have argued that in addition to focusing on major life changes it is important to also consider daily hassles in assessing the stressfulness of the person's environment. These include those often minor but still stressful situations and events such as having people cut in front of you in line, having trouble with a boss or teacher, being picked on by others, feeling lonely, and having too many responsibilities. Based on the assumed importance of assessing daily stressors, Kanner et al. (1981) have developed the Hassles Scale to assess these sorts of events, and Compas et al. (1985) chose to include a range of these types of events when developing their adolescent life events scale (Adolescents Perceived Events Scale), which was described earlier.

As discussed earlier, studies by Kanner et al. (1981) and others have provided preliminary data suggesting that measures of hassles are more highly correlated with indices of psychological adjustment than measures of major life events. It is also the case that the correlations between the Adolescent Perceived Events Scale (which assesses daily stressors in addition to major life changes) and measures of psychological adjustment are somewhat higher than those typically reported in the child/adolescent life events literature. A relevant but as yet unanswered question has to do with whether the higher correlations found with measures assessing hassles result from these being more relevant measures of stress or whether they result from a greater confounding of measures due to hassles more often being reflective of adjustment problems. Although there is currently much controversy regarding this point (see Dohrenwend & Shrout, 1985, and Lazarus et al., 1985, for a spirited debate regarding this issue), additional work will be necessary before any firm conclusions can be drawn. Clearly, many day-to-day events have the potential of being stressful and it seems important to assess them if we wish to have a comprehensive measure of stress. How to do this and at the same time avoid methodological confounds in life stress research is an important topic to be addressed in future work in this area.

The Problem of Retrospective Contamination

A second factor that contributes to the difficulty in interpreting child life stress studies has to do with the approaches investigators have taken in studying correlates of life stress. The bulk of child/adolescent life stress studies have been retrospective in nature. Often groups that have been shown to display some health problem, type of psychopathology, or adjustment problem have been compared with groups that do not display evidence of the condition or with some normative group, the dependent measure being some index of life change during the past year or so. Frequently the findings have suggested that diagnosed individuals show higher levels of life change than do comparison subjects. Although it may be tempting to conclude that the higher levels of life stress experienced by the diagnosed group contributed to their difficulty, there are problems with this conclusion. Parents of children with serious problems, or children themselves, may simply report more stressful life changes in an attempt to justify or account for their condition (a problem Brown, 1974, has referred to as "retrospective contamination"), or it may be that persons displaying some types of problems are simply biased toward recalling and/or reporting stressful life events (and in rating the stressfulness of events, if this is called for).

In retrospective studies that have attempted to document increased levels of life change that predate illness onset, there are still other problems that create difficulties in interpretation. For example, with problems such as childhood leukemia or juvenile rheumatoid arthritis, or with psychiatric problems of childhood, it may be difficult to determine exactly the time of onset. Studies that seek to assess life stress retrospectively over the year or so preceding diagnosis/referral may find higher levels of life stress in clinic groups simply because early manifestations of the child's condition contributed to the experiencing of certain life changes that were under the child's personal control.

The Directionality of Relationships

Other retrospective approaches to life stress research have involved obtaining measures of life stress and indices of health and/or adjustment at a particular point in time, often using all self-report measures. Subjects may be asked to complete a measure of life stress and measures of anxiety, depression, or some index of symptoms all at one point in time. Other studies have obtained measures of physical health over a specific period and have then asked subjects (or their parents) to report events experienced over the same period. Typically, significant relationships between life stress and such measures have been found. As suggested earlier, these findings are difficult to interpret, not only because the correlations may reflect a large degree of method variance (due to the use of all self-report indices) but also because it is often unclear whether life stress has resulted in anxiety, depression, psychiatric symptoms, or health difficulties or whether such characteristics simply result in an increased likelihood of experiencing life changes. Variables such as depression might also result in subjects being biased toward reporting more negative events and toward rating events experienced as more negative if self-ratings are involved. It is also conceivable that significant correlations are found because life stress and problems of health and adjustment covary with some other variable(s). Indeed, as was discussed in the previous chapter, Gersten et al. (1977) provided data suggesting that the commonly found relationship between life change and psychological impairment may result because both are related to "ongoing stressful life processes" (unhappy marriage of parents, low socioeconomic status, and so on). Although there are problems with this study that to some degree qualify these conclusions, as well as other research suggesting that obtained correlations between life stress and adjustment are not accounted for in terms of covariation with variables such as socioeconomic status (Gad & Johnson, 1980), the third variable problem must be viewed as a real one.

ADDRESSING THE ISSUE OF CAUSALITY

Given that, ultimately, it is desirable to reach the point at which causal *inferences* can be made and that we will continue to be unable to manipulate life stress experimentally, how does one proceed? It is likely that no study, regardless of how well designed, will be capable of providing data sufficient to justify the conclusion that a causal relationship exists. Again, it is impossible to "prove" the existence of a causal relationship from correlational data. However, by conducting studies designed to investigate and control for specific variables, it may be possible to accumulate a body of information that, when taken together, allows an inference of causality (or absence of causality) to be made with some justification. It is important that studies of this type be longitudinal (prospective) in nature, seek to eliminate the confounds of previous investigations (e.g., control for variables such as initial level of adjustment when assessing relationships between life change and later adjustment), and attempt to control for a range of other variables that might be predicted to contribute to both life stress and problems of health and adjustment (e.g., socioeconomic status).

Although the adequacy of the method has been debated (see Rogosa, 1980), one approach to addressing the issue of causality with correlational data has involved the use of cross-lagged correlation methodology. This quasi-experimental approach, described in detail by Kenny (1975), involves obtaining data on two variables of interest (life stress and adjustment, for example) at two points in time (Time 1; Time 2) and comparing the correlations among these variables across time.

Applied to research in the life stress area, correlations could be obtained between life stress scores and dependent variables obtained at Time 1 and at Time 2. These are the correlations that might be obtained in the typically correlational study. Correlations between life stress scores at Time 1 and Time 2 and between dependent measures at Time 1 and Time 2 can also be obtained. These provide information concerning the stability of measures over time. The remaining correlations are of primary interest in assessing the possibility (or nature) of a causal relationship. If a causal relationship exists so that life stress influences health and adjustment, one would expect to find life stress, assessed at Time 1 (controlling for initial health and adjustment status), to be significantly correlated with indices of health status and adjustment obtained at Time 2, and that this correlation would be greater than that obtained between health and adjustment, assessed at Time 1 (controlling for initial level of life stress) and life stress assessed at Time 2. A significant and larger correlation of the latter type would be more suggestive of a causal relationship in which health and adjustment influence subsequent life stress (a summary of the data obtained in such an analysis is depicted in Figure 5.1). This approach is of some value in investigating the *possibility* of causal relationship involving life stress, but it does have limitations. One is that it does not entirely eliminate the possibility that some additional variables, not considered in the analyses, may cause the two variables of interest (life stress and health status in this case) to covary. For a further discussion of this method, see Kenny (1975).

Although several studies conducted with adults have employed a cross-lagged panel methodology (or variations on this approach), and although these studies have often been suggestive of a causal relationship between life stress and outcome measures (see Antoni, 1985; Katz, 1982; Nelson & Cohen, 1983; Suls & Fletcher, 1985; Vossel & Froehlich, 1978, for example), fewer studies of this type have been conducted with children and adolescents. In fact, prospective studies of any type have been relatively rare in the child/adolescent literature. There are, however, data from recent investigations (Compas & Wagner, 1985; Compas et al., 1986; Swearingen & Cohen, 1985b) that are of relevance to the present discussion.

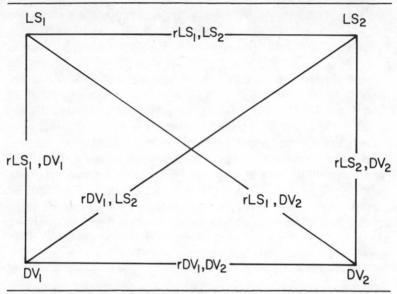

Figure 5.1   Example of cross-lag panel correlation design. From Johnson and Sarason (1979). Reproduced by permission.

In the Swearingen and Cohen study, 79 seventh and eighth graders were administered the Junior High Life Experiences Survey (Swearingen & Cohen, 1985a) along with the Child Depression Inventory and the State-Trait Anxiety Inventory for Children at two points in time, approximately five to six months apart. Simple zero-order correlations suggested that measures of negative (but not positive) life change were significantly correlated with indices of anxiety and depression when the cross-sectional data obtained at both Time 1 and Time 2 were considered. These correlations are quite similar to a number of those presented in Chapter 4 in indicating a significant link between negative change and depression and anxiety. The nature of these relationships, however, is clarified by subsequent multiple regression analyses based on the prospective data. When the relationship between negative change, assessed at Time 1, and subsequent level of anxiety and depression, assessed at Time 2, were considered (controlling for initial level of adjustment), no significant relationship was found. A relationship of this type would be expected if life stress resulted in problems of adjustment. Clearly, these findings do not support this type of causal relationship. Conversely, when regression analyses of the relationship between measures of anxiety and depression, obtained at Time 1, and negative change, obtained at Time 2, were considered (controlling for life events at Time 1), prior level of adjustment was found to be a significant predictor of subsequent negative change. To the extent that the findings of this study speak to the issue of a causal relationship, they suggest either that psychological distress contributes to the occurrence of negative events or that both negative change and distress result from some third variable.

Compas et al. (1986) conducted a similar study with 64 high school seniors making the transition from high school to college. Among other measures, these subjects were administered a 39-item life events measure (Newcomb et al., 1981) and the Hopkins Symptom Checklist (which provided a total symptom score) at three points in time. Time 1 data were obtained during an orientation meeting some three months prior to the time these subjects were to enter college. Time 2 data were obtained within one week of entry into college, and Time 3 data were obtained approximately three months later. Obtaining measures of life stress and adjustment at three points in time is quite unique in the life stress literature. The reason for it in this investigation related to the view that there may be certain times when individuals are more vulnerable to stress effects than others and specifically, that individuals are most vulnerable during major life transitions (such as entering college). Thus a major prediction was that the strongest relationship between life stress and total symptoms would be from Time 1 to Time 2, when the subjects had left home for college but had not yet had time to adjust to university life.

Overall correlations between measures of negative life change and the total symptom score of the Hopkins Checklist were found to be significant at each point in time. Regression analyses provided additional information regarding the nature of these relationships. Negative events (Time 1) were significantly related to Time 2 total symptom scores (even after controlling for initial level of adjustment). There was also a significant relationship between Time 1 total symptom scores and the experiencing of subsequent negative events at Time 2 (after controlling for initial level of life stress). Neither of these relationships was significant from Time 2 to Time 3.

Finding significant relationships between life stress and symptoms only at Time 2 provides general support for the hypothesis that the effects of life stress may be greatest during times of vulnerability associated with undergoing major life transitions. The other findings are somewhat less clear, as they suggest that life events are not only related to subsequent psychopathology but that initial level of adjustment is related to the later occurrence of life changes. These results are clearly not in accord with a direct causal relationship in which life stress causes psychological symptoms. Rather, they seem to suggest either that life stress and symptoms are both the result of some undetermined third variable or that there is a reciprocal relationship between stress and symptoms whereby life stress and level of adjustment serve to influence each other in a causal manner. Findings similar to these have also been provided by Compas and Wagner (1985), who obtained measures of life events (Adolescent Perceived Events Scale) and adjustment (Hopkins Symptom Checklist) at two points in time. As the life events measure employed here was composed of both major life events and daily hassles, these events were scored separately and dealt with separately in the data analysis. To summarize, daily hassles and symptoms were found to be reciprocally related across time (in the same manner as life stress and symptoms in the study cited above). Major life changes were not found to predict later symptoms, although initial level of adjustment was found to be predictive of later life events.

Although perhaps they raise more questions than they answer, these studies call into question the frequent assumption of a unidirectional causal relationship whereby stressful life events contribute to later psychopathology (we have no information from studies employing measures of health-related variables). To the extent that these preliminary studies, taken together, accurately reflect the nature of life stress-adjustment relationships (and we clearly need more research on this issue before deciding that this is so), they appear to tentatively suggest that although life events may in some instances contribute to problems of adjustment, the presence of psychological problems can also result in the experiencing of negative life changes. This view of a two-way relationship between life events and psychological symptoms is consistent with views of reciprocal determinism (Bandura, 1978) that see unidirectional causal relationships as being rare. From this perspective, individuals and the environment are seen as interacting in such a way that each is influenced by the other to a degree that makes it impossible to determine the causal effects of either the person on the environment or vice versa.

The studies cited above do not totally rule out the possibility that the apparent bidirectional relationship between life stress and adjustment, found in some studies, may result from the common influence of some undetermined variables that influence both life changes and adjustment. Such findings also need to be well replicated before drawing firm conclusions of any kind, especially as these findings with adolescents stand in contrast to several prospective studies with adults and college students that have yielded results consistent with a unidirectional relationship of the type expected. Clearly, additional prospective studies employing adequate measures of both stress and indices of health and adjustment are needed to address issues such as those raised here. In the meantime, any inferences regarding the causal effects of life events should be made with a degree of caution.

ON THE ROLE OF MODERATOR VARIABLES

People vary considerably in how they are affected by life events. In the case of adults, some get divorced, lose their jobs, experience financial hardships or death and illnesses in their family, and yet appear to suffer few apparent long-term physical or psychological consequences. Others seem to develop problems even in the face of relatively small amounts of life change. This differential response to adversity is likely to be seen in children and adolescents as well. An important issue for life event researchers concerns the nature of those social, physiological, and individual difference variables that lead to increased vulnerability or that play a protective role in the face of stress.

Although early life stress studies were usually designed simply to assess the relationships between life changes and other variables without considering how the relationship between life events and health-related outcomes might vary depending on other factors (thus ensuring the finding of less than robust correlations), more recent studies have increasingly focused on the role of moderator variables. This is especially true in the adult area. Here studies have found the relationship between life change and measures of health and/or adjustment to be moderated by variables such as social support (see Cohen & Wills, 1985), locus of control orientation (Johnson & Sarason, 1978), sensation or arousal seeking (Johnson, Sarason, & Siegel, 1979; Smith, Johnson, & Sarason, 1978), hardiness (Kobasa, 1979), and Type A-Type B behavioral styles (Kobasa, Maddi, & Zola, 1983), among others. Indeed, a major current focus in the adult literature is on delineating the nature of those variables that interact with life change in contributing to health-related outcomes (again assuming some sort of causal relationship).

Fewer child and adolescent studies have focused on the role of moderator variables, although studies of this type are beginning to appear in the literature with increasing frequency. A number of the studies considered in earlier chapters have provided support for the stress-buffering role of social supports (see Barrera, 1981; Lawrence & Russ, 1985; Sandler, 1980). Other studies have provided at least tentative support for several other presumed moderator variables, including parental attachment (Greenberg et al., 1983), Type A-Type B behavioral styles (Fontana & Dovidio, 1984), family routines (Boyce et al., 1973), locus of control (Brand et al., 1986), perceived competence (Lawrence & Russ, 1985), and sex of subject (Compas et al., 1985; Johnson & McCutcheon, 1980; Lawrence & Russ, 1985). Although these studies are few in number, they do provide good reason to believe that there are variables that may influence the degree to which children and adolescents, as well as adults, are affected by life stress.

Given our rather limited knowledge base in this area, further investigations of those variables that influence the child's response to stressful events are needed. It is only through an assessment of relevant moderator variables and consideration of these in designing research studies that we can begin to determine the degree to which, and under what conditions, life events are actually related to relevant aspects of child health and adjustment.

SUMMARY

In this chapter a range of conceptual and methodological issues that are important to consider in evaluating the life stress literature and in conducting research have been discussed. Among the issues discussed were several related to assessment. Questions dealt with whether life stress can best be conceptualized in terms of change per se or in terms of events that exert a negative impact on the individual, and with the optimal approach for assessing the desirability and weighting the impact of life changes. Related to the first issue, a number of child and adult studies were cited suggesting that negative life change is most highly correlated with problems of health and adjustment and that argue for the separate assessment of desirable and undesirable life changes. A case was also made for distinguishing between positive and negative life changes based on respondent's appraisals of events they have experienced. An argument was also made for the use of individualized impact ratings in weighting life events, but it was noted that the available research findings suggest that no method of weighting events is superior to a simple count of the number of events experienced (with a distinction being made between number of positive and negative events). In addition to these issues, other topics such as the time period over which life events should be assessed and who should provide life event data for child and adolescent studies were also discussed indicating that decisions made regarding each of these issues relate to the types of research findings obtained.

In addition to discussing issues related to assessment, it was pointed out that despite literature indicating numerous significant correlates of life change, the correlations reported are usually of relatively low magnitude, suggesting that life change accounts for only a small proportion of the variance in the dependent measures investigated. Reasons suggested for these low correlations included the inadequacy of life change measures, the fact that life change measures do not assess the entire range of stressors experienced by the individual, and the fact that many life event studies have not considered the role of variables that may moderate the relationship between life events and health/adjustment outcomes.

Not only are the correlations between life events and measures of health and adjustment of relatively low magnitude, but the nature of the relationships obtained is also difficult to interpret. As all life event studies are of a correlational nature and many have taken a retrospective approach, it is often unclear whether significant correlations mean that life events result in health/adjustment problems, whether health/adjustment problems result in increased life events, or alternately whether both are influenced by some other variable(s). The potential problem of biased reporting is also a ubiquitous concern in retrospective investigations.

Although a few prospective studies have sought to provide a more adequate basis for making inferences regarding the nature of life stress-dependent variable relationships, the available findings have not totally clarified this issue. Indeed, the results of some adolescent studies seem to suggest that life stress and adjustment-related variables may each exert an influence on the other in a reciprocal manner (or that the two are both the product of other ongoing processes). Drawing any conclusions from these studies must be done with caution, but the results clearly are not supportive of a simple unidirectional causal relationship in which life events exert a direct impact on health and/or adjustment.

As a final topic, attention was focused on the important role of moderator variables in life stress research. Citing research with both adults and children, it was indicated that the relationship between stressful life changes and measures of health and adjustment varies considerably as a function of both social and individual difference variables. A major task for future researchers involves determining the nature of those variables that make some children and adolescents more or less vulnerable to the effects of stress.

6

CHILD AND ADOLESCENT LIFE STRESS
Overview and Future Directions

The preceding chapters covered a range of issues relevant to the possible effects of life events on children and adolescents. In addition to reviewing ways professionals have attempted to conceptualize the nature of stress, a variety of measures designed to assess life changes in younger age groups have been considered, along with research regarding their adequacy. Separate chapters were devoted to reviewing research on the relationships between life changes and problems of physical health and psychological adjustment, as well as methodological issues that must be considered when interpreting research findings.

Although life event research with children and adolescents has lagged behind work with adults, there is currently a great deal of activity and interest in the area. This is reflected in the fact that several life event measures described here are in press at the time of this writing or have recently appeared in the literature, and that a large number of the studies reviewed also have only recently been published. Work in this area will continue at an accelerating pace during the next several years. Given this degree of interest and the likelihood that child/adolescent life events will continue to be a popular area of research, it seems appropriate to briefly summarize what is known in the field, and to comment on the direction that work in this area might take in the future.

First, what do we know? Methodological problems notwithstanding, it seems clear that the experiencing of life events is significantly related to a variety of health and adjustment problems experienced by children and adolescents. When factors such as the confounding of life events measures with measures of health and adjustment are controlled (to the extent possible), these relationships are not particularly strong. As has been discussed, the failure to find stronger relationships between life events and health/adjustment indices is most likely the result of several factors, including (a) general measurement problems, in particular the failure of studies to focus on those life changes that are most highly related to health/adjustment problems (e.g., negative life changes); (b) the fact that life change measures do not adequately assess many of the stressors experienced by children and adolescents; and (c) the fact that the majority of child/adolescent studies have not attended to variables that moderate the impact of life changes on individuals. Still another contributor to these relatively small correlations may have to do with the tendency of investigators to use nonstandardized measures, usually of unknown validity and reliability, to index health and adjustment problems. Nevertheless, although we cannot comment with certainty on the strength of the relationship between life events and problems of health and adjustment, the literature as a whole strongly suggests that a statistically significant relationship between these variables does in fact exist; life changes, especially those viewed as negative by the individual, *are* related to health-adjustment problems.

Despite this conclusion, we currently know less than we would like regarding the exact nature of these relationships. A few prospective studies have begun to address this issue; still, it is unclear whether the observed relationships result from the fact that life changes and health/adjustment problems both result from some common factor; whether life events cause health and adjustment problems; whether health and adjustment problems increase the probability of stressful life events; or whether life events and health/adjustment problems are related in some reciprocal manner. The best guess is that these relationships do not reflect a simple unidirectional causal relationship in which life events result in child/adolescent difficulties (as is usually assumed). Indeed, some studies suggest that life events and indices of health and adjustment may be reciprocally related such that each influences the other in a causal manner. However, research findings are too sparse to reach any firm conclusion at this time.

Without minimizing what has been gleaned from the rapidly increasing number of child/adolescent life event studies, the research findings to date can be summarized simply: Negative life events do seem to be related to certain health and adjustment problems of childhood, but we are not sure to what extent or in what way. Clearly, more work is needed.

Although some priorities for future research have been highlighted throughout the book, these areas as well as others not previously discussed warrant some additional comment. Several of these future directions are discussed in the sections to follow. Priorities related to research will be considered first. This will be followed by a discussion of an additional clinical priority, the need for the development of intervention approaches to help children and adolescents cope with stress.

PRIORITIES FOR FUTURE RESEARCH

Assessment Studies

Gains have been made in the area of child/adolescent life stress assessment, but the work is still in its infancy. Although the available data are more supportive of some measures than others, additional information is needed regarding the validity and reliability of virtually all of these measures (Compas, in press-a). Studies designed to determine optimal methods of weighting life events and the optimal time span for the assessment of life changes are needed, as are investigations designed to determine the unique contribution of daily stressors in assessing child/adolescent life changes. Regarding this latter point, it will be important to determine to what extent stronger correlations obtained with measures tapping daily hassles result from assessing a broader range of stressors as opposed to spuriousness due to the confounding of life event and health/adjustment measures. Although comparative studies of life event measures are currently nonexistent in the child/adolescent literature, investigations designed to compare assessment measures in terms of their relationship to relevant dependent measures are also needed.

Studies of Moderator Variables

An important priority concerns studies of those variables that influence the person's vulnerability (or lack of vulnerability) to stress. Investigations of moderator variables are common in the adult literature, but fewer studies of this type have been conducted with children and adolescents. Variables such as perceived competence, locus of control, family routines, Type A-Type B behavioral styles, and the like have been considered in isolated studies; however, the majority of investigations with younger age groups have focused on social support. Although social support certainly seems to be an important variable, the role of other variables as moderators of event impact should not be ignored. Additional studies, for example, might focus on variables such as individual differences in coping styles or on other factors such as child temperament characteristics (Thomas & Chess, 1977), as there is increasing evidence that temperament variables interact with environment factors to influence child adjustment (Plomin, 1983). Indeed, it seems likely that specific temperament characteristics that mirror the child's initial response to new situations (approach/withdrawal) and accommodation to novel situations over time (adaptability) may serve to influence the child's reactions to life change. It is also likely that many of the variables shown to be important in the adult literature are also of importance with children and adolescents. A focus on such variables should be a productive endeavor.

As more is learned regarding those variables that serve as moderators of life stress in children and adolescents, it is also important to consider the interactive (or additive) impact of these variables as they mediate the relationship between life events and health and adjustment. The importance of this approach is suggested by preliminary research with adults that has indicated that variables such as locus of control and social support may interact in this manner (e.g., support playing a stronger moderating role in individuals who see themselves as having control over environmental outcomes—Sandler & Lakey, 1982). The findings of an additional study (Lawrence & Russ, 1985) with adolescents, which suggests that the relationship between life changes and adjustment measures is stronger when measures of personal competence and social support are considered together than when either variable is considered alone, provides additional support for this view.

Although some preliminary work has been done, a detailed look at moderator variables relevant to younger age groups is a task for the future. As noted in Chapter 5, it is only through such studies, that we can begin to make statements regarding which individuals under which circumstances are most likely to be affected by stressful life changes.

Prospective Studies

A major problem with much of the work in this area relates to the retrospective nature of child/adolescent life stress investigations. Such studies may provide information regarding the correlates of life change, but they raise significant questions concerning the nature of the relationships obtained. The problem raised by the correlational and cross-sectional nature of this research have been commented on previously and will not be repeated here. Suffice to say that in the absence of well-controlled prospective investigations we will continue to be uncertain as to the nature of the relationships between life changes and child/adolescent problems. This lack of knowledge is likely to be a significant hindrance in decision making, because the focus of such important endeavors as prevention and intervention could differ depending on whether life events contribute to child/adolescent problems, these problems result in the experiencing of life events, or each influences the other in a reciprocal manner. It is certainly difficult to draw causal inferences from correlation data, but it remains essential that those working in the area continue to disentangle the nature of life event-dependent measure relationships such as those reported in the child and adolescent literature. Researchers such as Compas and his colleagues (see Compas & Wagner, 1985; Compas, Wagner, Slavin, & Vannatta, 1986) and Swearingen and Cohen (1985b) have made a start in this area; however, much more work will be needed before our questions concerning life event-health/adjustment relationships are fully answered.

Studies with Younger Children

Although an attempt has been made to consider what is known regarding child *and* adolescent life stress in the preceding chapters, a careful reading of these chapters will suggest that those working in the area have often paid much more attention to adolescents than to children. Especially neglected in this regard are younger children, below the age of 10 or so. With the exception of one form of the Coddington scale, all child/adolescent measures have been designed for use with older children and adolescents (Johnson & McCutcheon,

1980) or only for adolescents (Compas et al., 1985; Swearingen & Cohen, 1985; Tolor et al., 1983; Yeaworth et al., 1980). Measures such as the Life Events Checklist have been adapted for use with children as young as 5 to 7 years by having the child's parent indicate events the child has experienced and using judges' ratings of the desirability of events (obtained from independent judges [mothers]) to derive indices of positive and negative change (Katz, 1984). However, there are few data regarding the validity and reliability of the LEC when used in this way with children of this age. Given the limitations of the Coddington measure, discussed in Chapter 2, and the absence of other measures of demonstrated reliability and validity for younger children, a clear priority for the future seems to be the development of life event measures suitable for use with this age group.

Not only has less attention been given to the assessment of life changes in younger children but there have been fewer studies that have focused on the correlates of life events and the role of variables that may moderate the impact of life changes in this age group. Work in this area is needed, as are studies that attempt to assess the relationship between life changes and stress-related measures across age levels. Given the findings by Compas, Wagner, Slavin, and Vannatta (1986) supporting the view that individuals may be most vulnerable to the effects of life events during major life transitions (the transition from high school to college, in their study) and findings from other research that life changes are sometimes correlated with dependent measures at some ages but not at others (see Brand et al., 1986), studies designed to investigate the relationship between life stress and measures of health and adjustment in children undergoing normative life transitions (e.g., school entry, changing from elementary to junior high school, changing from junior high to high school) at different age levels may be particularly enlightening.

**Studies of Positive Change and
Positive Outcomes**

As Felner and his colleagues (Felner, 1984; Felner et al., 1983) have correctly pointed out, research on life events has been dominated by studies focusing on the potentially pathological effects of major life changes. This emphasis has resulted in primary attention being given to negative events and the negative outcomes (health problems, psychopathology) that may result from these events, with little consideration being given to the impact of positive events or the possibility that positive outcomes may sometimes result from negative changes if these are dealt with in an adaptive manner. Taking the perspective of one interested primarily in prevention as opposed to the possible precursors of psychopathology, Felner (1984, p. 137) has elaborated on this position as follows:

> If our concern is primarily with psychopathology, then the death of a parent, being expelled from school, or serious injury or illness may be more salient events than more predictable, and supposedly more positive events (such as school promotion or graduation). However, if prevention's focus is broadened to include the full range of potential adaptive outcomes, then positive events may be of equal salience. Although studies of life events have not found consistent associations between positive events and adaptive outcomes, there is no doubt that the way in which an individual or family masters adaptive challenges posed by such positive events as marriage, birth of a child, or receiving a desired promotion, can have important implications for their well-being, life satisfaction, and happiness. ... If primary prevention is concerned [both] with the enhancement of functioning and reduction of vulnerability, it seems clear that preventative efforts focused on life events need to develop a perspective which better attends to the potential for positive growth that may be associated with life events.

This point of view draws heavily on crisis theory as outlined by Caplan (1964), in that life events are viewed as crises to be resolved in either an adaptive or an maladaptive manner, with either outcome having implications both for the person's ability to resolve future crises and for later adaptive functioning. Those able to cope effectively with such events are more likely to come away with their coping abilities enhanced; the same events experienced by those who deal ineffectively may be more likely to lead to pathological outcomes (Felner, 1984).

Viewed in this manner, positive events are not simply occurrences that must be deleted from event counts if we are to find the strongest associations between life change measures and maladjustment. Rather, they are events that, if dealt with adaptively, may be importantly related to positive outcomes. Similarly, from this perspective, even some negative events might be seen as offering the potential for positive outcomes if dealt with adaptively.

Few life change studies have included measures designed to assess any kind of positive outcomes that might be associated with the experiencing of life changes, either positive or negative. Some studies, however, have found that increased levels of positive change are associated with lower rather than higher levels of depression (Swearingen & Cohen, 1985a), and lower rather than higher levels of maladjustment (Johnson & McCutcheon, 1980). Future investigations need to pay greater attention to the role of positive life events as changes that may have adaptive significance, and should include measures designed specifically to assess any positive effects that might accrue from experiencing such events. Consistent with this general point of view, it is important to examine the possibility that under some circumstances (for example, in individuals with good coping skills), even negative changes may relate to adaptive outcomes.

Studies of Greater Complexity

A common theme underlying many of the comments made in the preceding sections has to do with the need for greater complexity in life event research. At present, although we do not know all there is to know concerning the correlates of child/adolescent life change, it seems time to go beyond studies that simply seek to determine the relationship between some measure of life events on one hand and some measure of health and adjustment on the other. More likely to advance our knowledge in this area are investigations that seek to anwer more complex questions. A general framework for such questions might take these forms: What types of life events (e.g., daily hassles, pleasures, major life changes [positive and negative], events dealing with the family, school, peer relationships) relate to what types of outcomes (e.g., physical health problems, adjustment problems, enhanced functioning) in individuals displaying what types of characteristics (e.g., good versus poor social support, internal versus external perceptions of control, Type A-Type B behavioral styles), at what age levels (e.g., early childhood, older childhood, adolescence)? One might also add to this question regarding the type of relationships (e.g., causal-unidirectional, causal-reciprocal, noncausal-third-variable) that are found between life events and dependent measures (or independent measures, as the case may be) when the factors considered here are taken into account.

In considering the need for studies of greater complexity it will also be necessary to avoid making generalizations that are intuitively appealing and plausible but that may be inaccurate. To illustrate the point, most studies that have investigated moderator variables in children or adolescents have focused on the role of social support. For the most part, overall measures of support have been employed, apparently based on the notion that support per se is an important variable in buffering the effects of stress and increasing the likelihood of more positive outcomes in the face of stress. That this may be an erroneous assumption is suggested by the results of an investigation by Cauce, Felner, and Primavera (1982) that sought to distinguish meaningful dimensions of social support for adolescents from high-stress backgrounds. Through the use of factor-analytic procedures, Cauce et al. were able to identify three meaningful dimensions of support for this age group that accounted for some 95% of the total variance: family support (e.g., parents), formal support (e.g., teachers) and informal support (e.g., friends). These results were interpreted by the authors as providing support for the view that measures of social support that yield only a global index may "obscure important differences in the nature and differential adaptive influence of various sources of social support" (Felner, 1984, p. 144). Most relevant to the present discussion were the findings that type of social support was differentially related to adjustment measures. Although family support was significantly related to scholastic self-concept, peer support was found to be negatively related to school grades and school absences. The fact that under some circumstances social support may be related to negative outcomes has seldom been considered. Such findings suggest that even when studying what may *appear* to be unidimensional variables, there may be important distinctions to be made. Obviously no single life event study can attain the degree of complexity suggested by the present discussion, but it is important to incorporate aspects of this model if we are to advance our knowledge significantly regarding the possible impact of life events on children and adolescents.

MODIFYING THE IMPACT OF LIFE CHANGES:
ISSUES IN INTERVENTION

As we gain information concerning the effects of life events on children and adolescents, and those most likely to be affected by them, it becomes important to consider ways in which individuals can be taught to cope more effectively with such stressors. The development of programs to teach children and youth to cope with life stress is important from at least two perspectives: to help those who have already been exposed to high levels of life change deal with these stressors so as to minimize their effects on health and adjustment, and to help individuals develop adequate stress management skills for coping with future life changes in a preventive sense.

Unfortunately, although efforts have been made that are designed to help children cope with specific anxiety-based problems and other stressors such as phobias, dental fears, hospitalization, and stressful medical procedures (Morris & Kratochwill, 1983; Siegel, 1983), relatively little attention has been given to treatments designed to help children and adolescents cope with cumulative stressors of the type considered here (Compas, in press-b; Segal, 1983). The development of such intervention programs represents a goal for the future rather than a current reality, but it is possible to comment on the general direction intervention efforts might take.

Although not all have been widely used with children, a range of intervention approaches have been used within the context of stress and anxiety management programs for adults. Several of these approaches are discussed below in an attempt to highlight important components of a comprehensive stress management approach for working with children and adolescents experiencing high levels of life change.

Decreasing Physiological Arousal

It is generally agreed that anxiety and arousal are common characteristics of individuals under stress. Because of this, it is perhaps not surprising that most behaviorally oriented programs for dealing with stress and anxiety have included components for reducing physiological arousal. The primary approach has been training in progressive relaxation (Jacobsen, 1938; Wolpe, 1958). Relaxation training has most often been used within the context of traditional systematic desensitization in the treatment of specific phobias (Wolpe, 1958). It has also been used as a self-control technique (sometimes in combination with other treatment program components) in dealing with generalized anxiety (Goldfield, 1971; Richter, 1984). Using this technique as a self-control technique, the individual is likely to be trained in progressive relaxation, given instructions in how to use this newly acquired skill when confronting stressors, and provided with practice in its use. Here attention is likely to be placed on physical indicators of anxiety or muscle tension that can serve as cues for engaging in relaxation responses. Although most of the work on relaxation has been done with adults (again, usually within the context of desensitization treatments), it has also been used with children (see Richter, 1984). Most studies with children are characterized by methodological flaws; still, there is some evidence for the effectiveness of relaxation in dealing with anxiety-related problems, especially when relaxation training is accompanied by training in how and when to use this skill in real-life situations (Richter, 1984). More research with children is needed, but relaxation training, presented as a self-control technique, is likely to be of value in helping children cope with the increased levels of physiological arousal associated with experiencing life events.

Coping with Maladaptive Cognitions

In recent years increased attention has been given to the role of maladaptive cognitions (e.g., negative, self-defeating thoughts and self-statements) that contribute to and result from being exposed to stressful situations. As a result, approaches to stress management with adults have often incorporated procedures for dealing with these types of cognitions. Most representative of this approach is the Stress Inoculation Program developed by Meichenbaum (1975). Although this procedure involves several components, primary emphasis is placed on cognitive factors.

As described by Meichenbaum (1975), clients are first educated concerning the nature of stress reactions. They are told that stress responses involve two major elements: increased physiological arousal, and maladaptive thoughts. Basic assumptions underlying this approach are that in the presence of stressful stimuli, individuals engage in a variety of self-defeating thoughts (e.g., "I don't know what to do"; "I can't handle this situation"; "There's no way out of this") that increase the person's level of physiological arousal and decrease the likelihood of engaging in adaptive behavior, and that both physiological and cognitive reactions to stressful stimuli are capable of being modified.

After the educational phase of the program is completed, clients are taught a variety of coping behaviors to enable them to deal with stress. This involves training in progressive relaxation in order to help them cope with physiological arousal. Emphasis is also placed on helping the person develop a repertoire of adaptive self-statements that can be used when preparing for, confronting, and dealing with stressors (e.g., "Don't worry, that won't help anything"; "One step at a time, I can handle the situation"; "Don't try to eliminate the fear totally, just keep it manageable"; Meichenbaum, 1975, pp. 250-251). A final phase of the Stress Inoculation Program involves helping the person become proficient in using these coping skills by providing supervised practice in using these coping skills while dealing with actual stressors. In general, the approach is designed to help the person discern situations in which coping skills are called for (using increased levels of arousal and maladaptive cognitions as cues for coping) and to engage in coping behaviors designed to deal with those situations. This approach has been used primarily in helping individuals deal with specific stressors, but Meichenbaum has suggested that it may also be of value in helping people learn to cope with stressors they may encounter in the future, thus minimizing their effects (for a comprehensive overview of this approach, see Meichenbaum & Cameron, 1983).

Although this cognitively oriented approach has been developed for use with adults, the fact that other approaches to cognitive behavior modification (which are similar in many respects) have been shown to be useful with children displaying a range of problems (Kendall & Braswell, 1985) suggests that this sort of approach may be valuable in dealing with those maladaptive cognitions that contribute to stress-related problems of children and adolescents.

Training in Problem Solving

Experiencing major life events often results in problems other than the heightened anxiety and arousal (and maladaptive cognitions) that the coping skills program described above has been designed to deal with. Coping with life changes often involves making decisions as to how disruptions in one's life are to be dealt with and how the real problems resulting from life changes are to be resolved. This fact suggests that any comprehensive program for coping with life stress should probably include a significant problem-solving component. In this regard, problem-solving approaches such as those described by D'Zurilla and Goldfried (1971) with adults and by Spivack and Shure (1982) with children have much to offer. Learning to identify problem situations, reflectively generate and evaluate alternative solutions, and implement those that are most appropriate represent important coping skills that need to be developed by children and adolescents having to deal with significant life changes.

Mobilizing Personal Resources

Although limited, the research related to moderators of life stress also provides information that may have implications for helping children cope with stressful life changes. For example, several studies have suggested that children with good social support networks are less likely to suffer the adverse effects of life stress than those with lower levels of social support. These findings suggest that one way to help people cope with stress may be to increase their access to sources of support. As Dean and Lin (1977) have suggested, although it may not be possible for people to avoid experiencing certain stressful life events, it may be possible to find ways to help them mobilize supports within the community and thus, to some extent, minimize the effects of stress. It may also be possible, by teaching children and adolescents specific social skills, to increase the likelihood that they will themselves develop more protective social support networks that can be called on in times of stress.

Additional findings (with adults) suggest that the person's perceptions of the controllability of events may serve as a moderator of stress effects, and likewise suggest that interventions that serve to increase the individual's perception of control over environmental events may be especially useful. Such a sense of control may be fostered by behavioral coping skills programs that include components such as those described in the preceding sections.

Components of Coping: An Overview

Few programs are designed to help children and adolescents cope with cumulative life changes, and the development of any effective program must address issues such as those alluded to in the preceding sections. Clearly, it is important to find ways to help deal with the increased levels of physiological arousal that often results from exposure to stressful situations. Given the importance accorded the role of appraisal as it relates to the experiencing of stress, it also seems important to focus on those cognitive factors that influence one's appraisals of events and on those self-defeating or otherwise maladaptive cognitions that contribute to the overall level of stress experienced and to maladaptive behavior. Indeed, there is ample evidence from adult studies to suggest that these two components are of significant value in helping individuals cope with stress (Meichenbaum, 1975).

Training in problem solving and attempts to increase levels of social support may also be of value, as suggested by the results of a recent study by Marx, Somes, Garrity, Reeb and Maffeo (1983). In this study, which is one of the few investigations that has focused specifically on helping individuals cope with cumulative life changes, Marx et al. studied college students who were selected because they experienced high levels of life stress (which presumably put them at increased risk for the development of health problems). These subjects were assigned to either treatment or control conditions. Subjects who received treatment participated in a series of one-hour group sessions that focused on coping with life changes by emphasizing a problem-solving approach to dealing with stress within a supportive group atmosphere. Subjects in the control group received no treatment. The results suggested that subjects in the treatment groups displayed a significant decline in the number of illness episodes and number of disability days reported over the two semesters of study (as compared to the control group). Although these findings were with college students, they do support the notion that both social support and training in problem solving may be useful in helping individuals cope with stressful life changes.

Approaches such as those discussed here are likely to be of value in helping children cope with multiple stressors they confront during the process of growing up, but it may be necessary to consider other issues when dealing with certain major life transitions involving significant loss such as divorce and parental death. Thus although the procedures we have considered may be of value in helping the child cope with the range of life changes that may accompany events such as divorce and parental death (e.g., change in residence, change in school, loss of friends, surviving parent beginning work, remarriage of parent) that might otherwise contribute to adjustment problems (Felner, 1984; Felner et al., 1983, Hetherington, Cox, & Cox, 1985; Wallerstein, 1983, 1985), other intervention strategies may also be necessary in some cases. It is necessary to provide the child with a supportive atmosphere in which he or she can grieve over the loss of the parent and the breaking up of the family and to facilitate the child's dealing with the feelings of sadness, guilt, and anger associated with this loss and the circumstances surrounding it (King & Kleemeier, 1983; Koocher, 1983). In some instances this may involve the need for formal psychotherapy to help the child deal with the situation.

A Prototype for Child Stress Management Training

Although little attention has been given to the development of programs to help children cope with the multiple sources of stress and anxiety they experience, a recently developed program that contains a number of the desirable components described above has been developed by Pfohl (1980). This Children's Anxiety Management Program (CAMP) was designed to be implemented in the classroom over a period of 30 weeks (in 15- or 20-minute sessions two or three times per week) by a teacher, school psychologist, guidance counselor, or other professional. The program consists of five modules that are presented in an integrated fashion, so that each builds on the skills developed in earlier phases of the program. The overall objective is to help children develop skills for dealing with the diverse array of stressors they encounter in daily life.

In the first module, primary emphasis is placed on introducing the program and helping students learn something about the effects of stress and anxiety and how one can learn to cope with these. Activities such as class discussions about stressors each child has experienced and how different children have attempted to cope with stress are used to acquaint participants with the general area of stress and coping. Providing children with a general overview of the program is also a major goal of this initial module.

In the second module, the major focus is on training children in the use of progressive relaxation. Typical procedures are used: having the children alternately tense and relax muscles in various muscle groups, and accompanying this exercise with suggestions of relaxation and a focus on deep breathing. Children are asked to practice relaxation at home as well as in the training sessions and are instructed in the use of relaxation as an active coping skill for dealing with anxiety-arousing situations. Its use in this manner is encouraged throughout the program.

Module three represents the cognitive/psychological component of the CAMP program. Here the general purpose is to help participants learn a variety of cognitive skills that facilitate coping with stress and anxiety and to teach them how to integrate these skills with the use of relaxation. Emphasis is placed on the use of cognitive restructuring (to modify irrational and otherwise maladaptive ways of thinking), the development of problem-solving skills (to help participants learn to size up the problems, generate alternative solutions, evaluate and choose among these, and implement a desirable course of action), and the use of imagery (in order to provide cognitive rehearsal of coping successfully with problems). As in the case of earlier modules, an attempt is made to teach these skills within the context of group discussions and to integrate what is taught with what has already been learned.

Module four is described as the social/behavioral component of the program, in which children are encouraged to practice the coping skills they have learned while dealing with actual stressors. For example, children may be asked to choose a number of anxiety-arousing situations to deal with (e.g., sharing a sad event) and use the coping skills they have learned to cope with any anxiety experienced. In some instances children may be used to model these coping responses for others in the group. To encourage the use of these skills in daily life, children are also asked to keep records of the number of times they have used these skills to deal with problems they encounter outside training sessions. Attention is also given to assertiveness training, in order to facilitate children's ability to actively carry out effective coping behaviors that involve social interaction. Emphasis is placed on developing these skills through the use of modeling, role-playing, imagery rehearsal, and practice in actual stressful situations.

The final portion of the program is designed to promote generalization and durability of the skills that have been learned during the program. In this regard, additional emphasis is placed on using coping skills whenever the child confronts stressful situations. At the end of the program there are regular meetings to encourage the continued use of these skills, as well as "booster sessions" offered on a monthly basis.

This is a very intensive and comprehensive program involving many of the components that have proven useful in stress management programs for adults. It addresses at once the physiological, cognitive, and behavioral effects of stressors and focuses on the development of coping skills at each of these levels. Furthermore, rather than assuming generalization of treatment effects outside training sessions, the program is designed to promote actively generalization and maintenance of coping skills. Although little information is currently available regarding the effectiveness of this program, it is likely to be useful in helping children cope with the range of stressors they confront in daily life. Studies designed to determine the effectiveness of such a program with children who are at risk for health/adjustment problems due to experiencing high levels of negative life changes (and who display characteristics that make them more vulnerable to the effects of these changes) would be especially worthwhile.

SUMMARY

This chapter was an overview of what is currently known about the relationship between child/adolescent life changes and problems of health and adjustment and included comments on some profitable directions for future work. The literature, taken together, provides considerable support for a statistically significant relationship between the experiencing of cumulative life changes (especially negative ones) and problems of health and adjustment. Despite this fact, the magnitude of the life stress-health/adjustment relationships found in most studies is usually relatively small (suggesting that measures of life stress by themselves are not likely to be especially predictive), and the nature of the relationships obtained are usually unclear. In considering the limited findings that are available, the assumption of a simple, straightforward unidirectional relationship in which life stress causes child/adolescent problems may be an oversimplification. However, more data are needed.

In considering priorities for future research, studies of several types are needed. These include additional studies of the adequacy of existing life change measures, studies of variables that may moderate the impact of life changes, studies dealing specifically with younger children, and studies that focus more specifically on the correlates of positive life changes. Especially emphasized was the need for additional studies of a prospective nature to clarify better the nature of the relationship between life changes and problems of child/adolescent health and adjustment and studies of greater complexity than those currently found in the literature.

Finally, relatively little attention has been given to the development of interventions designed to help children and adolescents cope with cumulative life changes. To the extent that the findings from future research documents the impact of life stress on the health and adjustment of children and youth, it is essential that increased attention be given to the development of such programs.

REFERENCES

Antoni, M. H. (1985). Temporal relationship between life events and two illness measures: A cross-lagged panel analysis. *Journal of Human Stress, 11,* 21-28.

Bandura, A. (1987). The self system in reciprocal determinism. *American Psychologist, 33,* 344-358.

Barrera, M. (1981). Social support's role in the adjustment of pregnant adolescents: Assessment issues and findings. In B. H. Gottleib (Ed.), *Social networks and social support in community mental health.* Beverly Hills, CA: Sage.

Baum, A., Grunberg, N. E., & Singer, J. E. (1982). The use of psychological and neuroendocrinological measurements in the study of stress. *Health Psychology, 1,* 217-236.

Beautrais, A. L., Fergusson, D. M., & Shannon, F. T. (1982). Life events and childhood morbidity: A prospective study. *Pediatrics, 70,* 935-940.

Bedell, J. R., Giordani, B., Amour, J. L., Tavormina, J., & Boll, T. (1977). Life stress and the psychological and medical adjustment of chronically ill children. *Journal of Psychosomatic Research, 21,* 237-242.

Boyce, T. W., Jensen, E. W., Cassell, J. C., Collier, A. M., Smith, A. H., & Raimey, C. T. (1973). Influence of life events and family routines on childhood respiratory tract illness. *Pediatrics, 60,* 609-615.

Bradley, C. (1979). Life events and the control of diabetes mellitus. *Journal of Psychosomatic Research, 23,* 159-162.

Bramwell, S. T., Wagner, N. N., Masuda, M., & Holmes, T. H. (1975). Psychosocial factors in athletic injuries. *Journal of Human Stress, 1,* 6-20.

Brand, A. H., & Johnson, J. H. (1982). Note on the reliability of the Life Events Checklist. *Psychological Reports, 50,* 1274.

Brand, A. H., Johnson, J. H., & Johnson, S. B. (1986). *The relationship between life stress and diabetic control in insulin-dependent diabetic children and adolescents.* Unpublished Manuscript, University of Florida.

Brown, G. W. (1974). Meaning, measurement, and stress of life events. In B. S. Dohrenwend & B. P. Dohrenwend (Eds.), *Stressful life events: Their nature and effects.* New York: John Wiley.

Bruns, C., & Geist, C. S. (1984). Stressful life events and drug use among adolescents. *Journal of Human Stress, 9,* 135-139.

Caplan, G. (1964). *Principles of preventative psychiatry.* New York: Basic Books.

Carranza, E. (1972). *A study of the impact of life changes on high school teacher performance in the Lansing school district as measured by the Holmes and Rahe Schedule of Recent Experiences.* Unpublished doctoral dissertation, Michigan State University.

Cauce, A. M., Felner, R. D., & Primavera, J. (1982). Social support systems in high risk adolescents: Structural components and adaptive impact. *American Journal of Community Psychology, 10,* 417-428.

Chan, D. A., & Perry, M. A. (1981). *Child abuse: Discriminating factors toward a positive outcome.* Paper presented at the biennial meeting of the Society for Research in Child Development, Boston.

Chase, H. P., & Jackson, G. G. (1981). Stress and sugar control in children with insulin-dependent diabetes mellitus. *Journal of Pediatrics, 98,* 1011-1013.

Coddington, R. D. (1972a). The significance of life events as etiological factors in the diseases of children: A study of a normal population. *Journal of Psychosomatic Research, 16,* 205-213.

Coddington, R. D. (1972b). The significance of life events as etiologic factors in the diseases of children: A survey of professional workers. *Journal of Psychosomatic Research, 16,* 7-18.

Coddington, R. D. (1979). Life events associated with adolescent pregnancies. *Journal of Clinical Psychiatry, 40,* 180-185.

Coddington, R. D., & Troxell, J. R. (1980). The effect of emotional factors on football injury rates: A pilot study. *Journal of Human Stress, 6,* 3-5.

Cohen, S., & Wills, T. A. (1985). Stress, social support, and the buffering hypothesis. *Psychological Bulletin, 98,* 310-357.

Cohen-Sandler, R., Berman, A. L., & King, R. A. (1982). Life stress and symptomatology: Determinants of suicidal behavior in children. *Journal of the American Academy of Child Psychiatry, 21,* 178-186.

Compas, B. E. (in press-a). Stress as life events during childhood and adolescence. *Clinical Psychology Review.*

Compas, B. E. (in press-b). Coping with stress during childhood and adolescence. *Psychological Bulletin.*

Compas, B. E. (1986). Personal communication, July 30.

Compas, B. E., Davis, G. E., Forsythe, C. J., & Wagner, B. M. (1985). *Assessment of major and daily life events during adolescence: The Adolescent Perceived Events Scale.* Unpublished manuscript, University of Vermont.

Compas, B. E., Davis, G. E., & Forsythe, C. J. (1985). Characteristics of life events during adolescence. *American Journal of Community Psychology, 13,* 677-691.

Compas, B. P., Slavin, L. A., Wagner, B. M., & Vannatta, K. (1985). *Relationship of life events and social support with psychological dysfunction among adolescents.* Unpublished manuscript, University of Vermont.

Compas, B. E., & Wagner, B. M. (1985). *Reciprocal relationships of life events and daily hassles with psychological symptoms: A prospective study.* Paper presented at the annual convention of the American Psychological Association, Los Angeles.

Compas, B. E., Wagner, B. M., Slavin, L. A., & Vannatta, K. (1986). A prospective study of life events, social support, and psychological symptomatology during the transition from high school to college. *American Journal of Community Psychology, 14,* 241-257.

Cowen, E. L., Trost, M. A., Lorion, R. P., Door, D., Izzo, L. D., & Issacson, R. U. (1975). *New ways in school mental health: Early detection and prevention of school maladaption.* New York: Human Sciences Press.

Cowen, E. L., Weissberg, R. P., & Guare, J. (1984). Differentiating attributes of children referred to a school mental health program. *Journal of Abnormal Child Psychology, 12,* 397-410.

D'Zurilla, T. J., & Goldfried, M. R. (1971). Problem solving and behavior modification. *Journal of Abnormal Psychology, 78,* 107-126.

Dally, P. J. (1969). *Anorexia nervosa.* New York: Grune & Stratton.

De Araujo, G., Van Arsdel, P. O., Holmes, T. H., & Dudley, D. L. (1973). Life change, coping ability and chronic intrinsic asthma. *Journal of Psychosomatic Research, 17,* 359-363.

Dean, A., & Lin, N. (1977). The stress-buffering role of social support. *Journal of Nervous and Mental Disease, 165,* 403-417.

Dekker, D. J., & Webb, J. T. (1974). Relationships of the social readjustment rating scale to psychiatric patient status, anxiety, and social desirability. *Journal of Psychosomatic Research, 18,* 125-130.

DeLongis, A., Coyne, J. C., Dakof, G., Folkman, S., & Lazarus, R. S. (1983). Relationship of daily hassles, uplifts, and major life events to health status. *Health Psychology, 1,* 119-136.

Derogatis, L. R. (1977). *SCL-90: Administration, scoring and procedures manual for the R version.* Baltimore: Author.

Derogatis, L. R., Lipman, R. S., Rickels, K., Uhlenhuth, E. H., & Covi, L. (1974). The Hopkins Symptom Checklist. *Pharmacopsychiatry, 7,* 79-110.

Dohrenwend, B. P., & Shrout, P. E. (1985). "Hassles" in the conceptualization and measurement of life stress variables. *American Psychologist, 40,* 780-785.

Dohrenwend, B. S. (1973). Life events as stressors: A methodological inquiry. *Journal of Health and Social Behavior, 14,* 167-175.

Dohrenwend, B. S., & Dohrenwend, B. P. (1974). Overview and prospects for research on stressful life events. In B. S. Dohrenwend & B. P. Dohrenwend (Eds.), *Stressful life events: Their nature and effects.* New York: Wiley.

Dohrenwend, B. S., Krasnoff, L., Askenasy, A. R., & Dohrenwend, B. P. (1978). Exemplification of a method for scaling life events: The PERI Life Events Scale. *Journal of Health and Social Behavior, 19,* 225-239.

Edwards, M. K. (1971). *Life crises and myocardial infarction.* Unpublished master's thesis, University of Washington, Seattle.

Egeland, B., Breitenbucher, M., & Rosenberg, D. (1980). Prospective study of the significance of life stress in the etiology of child abuse. *Journal of Consulting and Clinical Psychology, 48,* 195-205.

Felner, R. D. (1984). Vulnerability in childhood: A preventative framework for understanding children's efforts to cope with life stress and transitions. In M. C. Roberts & L. Peterson (Eds.), *Prevention of problems in childhood.* New York: John Wiley.

Felner, R. D., Farber, S. S., & Primavera, J. (1980). Children of divorce, stressful life events, and life transitions: A framework for preventative efforts. In R. H. Price, R. F. Ketterer, B. C. Bader & J. Monahan (Eds.), *Prevention in mental health: Research, policy and practice.* Beverly Hills, CA: Sage.

Felner, R. D., Farber, S. S., & Primavera, J. (1983). Transitions and stressful life events: A model for primary prevention. In R. D. Felner, L. A. Jason, J. N. Moritsugu & S. S. Farber (Eds.), *Preventative psychology: Theory, research, and practice.* New York: Pergamon.

Felner, R. D., Stolberg, A., & Cowen, E. L. (1975). Crisis events and school mental health referral patterns of young children. *Journal of Consulting and Clinical Psychology, 43,* 305-310.

Ferguson, W. (1981). Gifted adolescents, stress and life changes. *Adolescence, 16,* 973-985.

Fitts, A. W. (1965). *Tennessee Self Concept Inventory.* Nashville: Counselor, Recordings, & Tests.

Fontana, A., & Dovidio, J. F. (1984). The relationship between stressful life events and school related performances of Type A and Type B adolescents. *Journal of Human Stress, 10,* 50-54.

Friedman, M., & Rosenman, R. H. (1974). *Type A behavior and your heart.* New York: Knopf.

Friedrich, W., Reams, R., & Jacobs, J. (1982). Depression and suicidal ideation in early adolescents. *Journal of Youth and Adolescence, 11,* 403-407.

Gad, M. T., & Johnson, J. H. (1980). Correlates of adolescent life stress as related to race, SES, and levels of perceived social support. *Journal of Clinical Child Psychology, 9,* 13-16.

Gaines, R., Sandgrund, A., Green, A. H., & Power, E. (1978). Etiological factors in child maltreatment: A multivariate study of abusing, neglecting and normal mothers. *Journal of Abnormal Psychology, 87,* 531-540.

Garmezy, N. (1983). Stressors in childhood. In N. Garmezy & M. Rutter (Eds.), *Stress, coping, and development in children.* New York: McGraw-Hill.

Gersten, E. (1976). A health resources inventory: The development of a measure of the personal and social competence of primary grade children. *Journal of Consulting and Clinical Psychology, 44,* 775-786.

Gersten, J. C., Langer, T. S., Eisenberg, J. G., & Orzeck, L. (1974). Child behavior and life events: Desirable change or change per se. In B. S. Dohrenwend & B. P. Dohrenwend (Eds.), *Stressful life events: Their nature and effects.* New York: John Wiley.

Gersten, J. C., Langer, T. S., Eisenberg, J. G., & Simcha-Fagan, O. (1977). An evaluation of the etiological role of stressful life-change events in psychological disorders. *Journal of Health and Social Behavior, 18,* 228-244.

Gilbert, B. (1985). *Physiological responsivity to venipuncture and speech giving in insulin-dependent diabetic adolescents at two levels of diabetic control and their nondiabetic peers.* Unpublished doctoral dissertation, University of Florida.

Glass, D. C. (1977). *Behavior patterns, stress, and coronary disease.* Hillsdale, NJ: Erlbaum.

Goldfried, M. R. (1971). Systematic desensitization as training in self control. *Journal of Consulting and Clinical Psychology, 37,* 228-234.

Gorsuch, R. L., & Key, M. K. (1974). Abnormalities of pregnancy as a function of anxiety and life stress. *Psychosomatic Medicine, 36,* 352-361.

Gortmaker, S. L., Eckenrode, J., & Gore, S. (1982). Stress and the utilization of health services: A time series and cross-sectional analysis. *Journal of Health and Social Behavior, 23,* 25-28.

Grant, I., Kyle, G. C., Teichman, A., & Mendels, J. (1974). Recent life events and diabetes in adults. *Psychosomatic Medicine, 36,* 121-128.

Grant, I., Sweetwood, H. L., Yager, J., & Gerst, M. (1981). Quality of life in relation to psychiatric symptoms. *Archives of General Psychiatry, 38,* 335-339.

Green, W. A. (1952). *Psychological factors and reticuloendothelial disease. III. Further observations on psychological and somatic manifestations in patients with lymphomas and leukemia.* Paper presented at the annual meeting of the American Psychosomatic Society, Chicago (March).

Green, W. A. (1954). Psychological factors and reticuloendothelial disease: Preliminary observations on a group of males with lymphomas and leukemias. *Psychosomatic Medicine, 16,* 220-230.

Green, W. A., Young, L. E., Swisher, S. N., & Miller, G. (1955). Psychological factors and reticuloendothelial disease: Observations on a group of females with lymphomas and leukemias. *Psychosomatic Medicine, 18,* 284-303.

Greenberg, M. T., Siegel, J. M., & Leitch, C. J. (1983). The nature and importance of attachment relationships to parents and peers during adolescence. *Journal of Youth and Adolescence, 12,* 373-386.

Greene, J. W., Walker, L. S., Hickson, G., & Thompson, J. (1985). Stressful life events and somatic complaints in adolescents. *Pediatrics, 75,* 19-22.

Harris, P. W. (1972). *The relationship of life change to academic performance among selected college freshmen at varying levels of college readiness.* Unpublished doctoral dissertation, East Texas State University.

Harter, S. (1982). The perceived competence scale for children. *Child Development, 53,* 87-97.

Heisel, J. S., Ream, S., Raitz, R., Rappaport, M., & Coddington, R. D. (1973). The significance of life events as contributing factors in the diseases of children. *Behavioral Pediatrics, 83,* 119-123.

Hetherington, E. M., Cox, M., & Cox, R. (1985). Long-term effects of divorce and remarriage on the adjustment of children. *Journal of the American Academy of Child Psychiatry, 24,* 518-530.

Hodges, K., Kline, J. J., Barbero, G., & Flanery, R. (1984). Life events occurring in families of children with recurrent abdominal pain. *Journal of Psychosomatic Research, 28,* 185-188.

Holmes, T. H. (1979). Development and application of a quantitative measure of life change magnitude. In J. E. Barrett (Ed.), *Stress and mental disorder.* New York: Raven Press.

Holmes, T. H., & Masuda, M. (1974). Life change and illness susceptibility. In B. S. Dohrenwend & B. P. Dohrenwend (Eds.), *Stressful life events: Their nature and effects.* New York: John Wiley.

Holmes, T. H., & Rahe, R. H. (1967). The social readjustment rating scale. *Journal of Psychosomatic Research, 11,* 213-218.

Hotaling, G. T., Atwell, S. G., & Linsky, A. S. (1978). Adolescent life change and illness: A comparison of three models. *Journal of Youth and Adolescence, 7,* 393-403.

Hudgens, R. W. (1974). Personal catastrophe and depression: A consideration of the subject with respect to medically ill adolescents, and a requiem for retrospective life-event studies. In B. S. Dohrenwend & B. P. Dohrenwend (Eds.), *Stressful life events: Their nature and effects.* New York: John Wiley.

Jacobs, T. J., & Charles, E. (1980). Life events and the occurrence of cancer in children. *Psychosomatic Medicine, 42,* 11-24.

Jacobsen, E. (1938). *Progressive relaxation.* Chicago: University of Chicago Press.

Jemmott, J. B., & Locke, S. E. (1984). Psychosocial factors, immunologic mediation, and human susceptibility to infectious diseases: How much do we know? *Psychological Bulletin, 95,* 78-108.

Jenkins, C. D., Hurst, M. W., & Rose, R. M. (1979). Life changes: Do people really remember? *Archives of General Psychiatry, 36,* 379-384.

Johnson, J. H. (1982). Life events as stressors in childhood and adolescence. In B. Lahey & A. Kazdin (Eds.), *Advances in clinical child psychology.* New York: Plenum.

Johnson, J. H., & McCutcheon, S. M. (1980). Assessing life stress in older children and adolescents: Preliminary findings with the Life Events Checklist. In I. G. Sarason & C. D. Spielberger (Eds.), *Stress and Anxiety.* Washington, DC: Hemisphere.

Johnson, J. H., & Overall, J. E. (1973). Factor analysis of the Psychological Screening Inventory. *Journal of Consulting and Clinical Psychology, 41,* 57-60.

Johnson, J. H., & Sarason, I. G. (1978). Life stress, depression and anxiety: Internal-external control as a moderator variable. *Journal of Psychosomatic Research, 22,* 205-208.

Johnson, J. H., & Sarason, I. G. (1979a). Recent developments in research on life stress. In V. Hamilton & D. Warburton (Eds.), *Human stress and cognition: An information processing approach.* London: John Wiley.

Johnson, J. H., & Sarason, I. G. (1979b). Moderator variables in life stress research. In I. G. Sarason & C. D. Spielberger (Eds.), *Stress and anxiety.* Washington, DC: Hemisphere.

Johnson, J. H., Sarason, I. G., & Siegel, J. M. (1979). Arousal seeking as a moderator of life stress. *Perceptual and Motor Skills, 49,* 665-666.

Justice, B., & Duncan, D. F. (1976). Life crisis as a precursor to child abuse. *Public Health Reports, 91,* 110-115.

Kagan, J. (1983). Stress and coping in early development. In N. Garmezy & M. Rutter (Eds.), *Stress, coping, and development in children.* New York: McGraw-Hill.

Kanner, A. D., Coyne, J. C., Schaefer, C., & Lazarus, R. S. (1981). Comparison of two modes of stress measurement: Daily hassles and uplifts versus major life events. *Journal of Behavioral Medicine, 4,* 1-19.

Katz, D. L. (1984). *The relationship between life stress and adjustment as a function of child temperament.* Unpublished master's thesis, University of Florida.

Katz, J. F. (1982). *Life stress and psychological change: A cross-lagged panel analysis.* Paper presented at the annual meeting of the American Psychological Association, Washington, DC.

Kendall, P. C., & Braswell, L. (1985). *Cognitive behavioral therapy for impulsive children.* New York: Guilford.

Kenny, D. A. (1975). Cross-lagged panel correlation: A test for spuriousness. *Psychological Bulletin, 82,* 887-903.

King, H. E., & Kleemeier, C. P. (1983). The effects of divorce on parents and children. In C. E. Walker & M. C. Roberts (Eds.), *Handbook of clinical child psychology.* New York: John Wiley.

Kobasa, S. C. (1979). Stressful life events, personality, and health: An inquiry into hardiness. *Journal of Personality and Social Psychology, 37,* 1-11.

Kobasa, S. C., Maddi, S. R., & Zola, M. A. (1983). Type A and Hardiness. *Journal of Behavioral Medicine, 6,* 41-51.

Koocher, G. P. (1983). Grief and loss in childhood. In C. E. Walker & M. C. Roberts (Eds.), *Handbook of clinical child psychology.* New York: John Wiley.

Kovacs, M. (1980). Rating scales to assess depression in school-aged children. *Acta Paedopsychiatrica, 46,* 305-315.

Lal, N., Ahuja, R. C., & Madhukar, A. (1982). Life events in hypertensive patients. *Journal of Psychosomatic Research, 26,* 441-445.

Langer, T. (1962). A twenty-two item screening scale of psychiatric symptoms indicating impairment. *Journal of Health and Social Behavior, 3,* 269-276.

Lauer, R. H. (1973). The social readjustment scale and anxiety. *Journal of Psychosomatic Research, 17,* 171-174.

Lawrence, D. B., & Russ, S. W. (1985). *Mediating variables between life stress and symptoms among young adolescents.* Paper presented at the annual meeting of the American Psychological Association, Los Angeles.

Lazarus, R. S. (1966). *Psychological stress and the coping process.* New York: McGraw-Hill.

Lazarus, R. S., DeLongis, A., Folkman, S., & Gruen, R. (1985). Stress and adaptational outcomes: The problem of confounded measures. *American Psychologist, 40,* 770-779.

Lazarus, R. S., & Folkman, S. (1985). *Stress, appraisal, and coping.* New York: Springer.

Lazarus, R. S., & Launier, R. (1978). Stress-related transactions between persons and environment. In L. A. Pervin & M. Lewis (Eds.), *Perspectives in interactional psychology.* New York: Plenum.

Leaverton, D. R., White, C. A., McCormick, C. R., Smith, P., & Sheikholislam, B. (1980). Parental loss antecedent to childhood diabetes mellitis. *Journal of the American Academy of Child Psychiatry, 19,* 678-689.

Levenson, H., Hirschfeld, M. L., Hirschfeld, A., & Dzubay, B. (1983). Recent life events and accidents: The role of sex differences. *Journal of Human Stress, 9,* 4-8.

Lorion, R. P., Cowen, E. L., & Caldwell, R. A. (1975). Normative and parametric analyses of school maladjustment. *American Journal of Community Psychology, 3,* 293-301.

Lundberg, V., Theorell, T., & Lind, E. (1975). Life changes and myocardial infarction: Individual differences in life change scaling. *Journal of Psychosomatic Research, 19,* 27-32.

Maloney, M. J., & Klykylo, W. M. (1983). An overview of anorexia nervosa, bulimia, and obesity in children and adolescents. *Journal of the American Academy of Child Psychiatry, 22,* 99-107.

Marx, M. B., Somes, G. W., Garrity, T. F., Reeb, A. C., & Maffeo, P. A. (1984). The influence of a supportive, problem-solving group intervention in the health status of students with great recent life change. *Journal of Psychosomatic Research, 28,* 275-278.

Mason, J. W. (1975). A historical view of the stress field. *Journal of Human Stress, 1,* 22-36.

McCubbin, H. I., Needle, R. H., & Wilson, M. (1985). Adolescent health risk behaviors: Family stress and adolescent coping as critical factors. *Family Relations, 34,* 51-62.

McCubbin, H. I., Patterson, J. M., & Wilson, L. R. (1982). Family inventory of life events and changes. In D. Olson, H. I. McCubbin, H. Barnes & A. Larsen (Eds.), *Family inventories: Inventories used in a national survey of families across the family life cycle.* St. Paul, MN: Author.

Meichenbaum, D. (1975). A self-instructional approach to stress management: A proposal for stress inoculation training. In C. D. Spielberger & I. G. Sarason (Eds.), *Stress and anxiety.* Washington, DC: Hemisphere.

Meichenbaum, D., & Cameron, R. (1983). Stress inoculation training. In D. Meichenbaum & M. E. Jeremko (Eds.), *Stress reduction and prevention.* New York: Plenum.

Meyer, R. J., & Haggerty, R. J. (1962). Streptococcal infections in families. *Pediatrics, 29,* 539-549.

Monaghan, J. H., Robinson, J. O., & Dodge, J. A. (1979). The Children's Life Events Inventory. *Journal of Psychosomatic Research, 23,* 63-68.

Monroe, S. M. (1982). Life events assessment: Current practices, emerging trends. *Clinical Psychology Review, 2,* 435-453.

Monroe, S. M., Bellack, A. S., Hersen, M., & Himmelhoch, J. M. (1983). Life events, symptom course and treatment outcome in unipolar depressed women. *Journal of Consulting and Clinical Psychology, 51,* 604-615.

Moos, R. (1974). *Preliminary manual for the Family Environment Scale.* Palo Alto, CA: Consulting Psychologists Press.

Morris, R., & Kratochwill, T. R. (1983). *Treating children's fears and phobias.* New York: Pergamon.

Mueller, D. P., Edwards, D. W., & Yarvis, R. M. (1977). Stressful life events and psychiatric symptomatology: Change or undesirability. *Journal of Health and Social Behavior, 18,* 307-317.

Mullins, L. L., Siegel, L. J., & Hodges, K. (1985). Cognitive problem solving and life event correlates of depressive symptoms in children. *Journal of Abnormal Child Psychology, 13,* 305-314.

Myers, J. K., Lindenthal, J. J., & Pepper, M. P. (1974). Social class, life events, and psychiatric symptoms: A longitudinal study. In B. S. Dohrenwend & B. P. Dohrenwend (Eds.), *Stressful life events: Their nature and effects.* New York: John Wiley.

Nelson, D., & Cohen, L. (1983). Locus of control perceptions and the relationship between life stress and psychological disorder. *American Journal of Community Psychology, 11,* 705-722.

Newcomb, M. D., Huba, G. J., & Bentler, P. M. (1981). A multidimensional assessment of stressful life events among adolescents: Derivation and correlates. *Journal of Health and Social Behavior, 22,* 400-415.

Nuckolls, K. B., Cassell, J., & Kaplan, B. H. (1972). Psychosocial assets, life crisis and the prognosis of pregnancy. *American Journal of Epidemiology, 95,* 431-441.

Padilla, E. R., Rohsenow, D. J., & Bergman, A. B. (1976). Predicting accident frequency in children. *Pediatrics, 58,* 223-226.

Pantell, R. H., & Goodman, B. W. (1983). Adolescent chest pain: A prospective study. *Pediatrics, 71,* 881-886.

Patterson, J. M., & McCubbin, H. I. (1983). The impact of family life events and changes on the health of a chronically ill child. *Family Relations: Journal of Applied Family and Child Studies, 32,* 255-264.

Paykel, E. S. (1974). Life stress and psychiatric disorder: Applications of the clinical approach. In B. S. Dohrenwend & B. P. Dohrenwend (Eds.), *Stressful life events: Their nature and effects.* New York: John Wiley.

Pfohl, W. (1980). Children's anxiety management program: A broad-based behavioral program teaching children to cope with stress and anxiety. *Dissertation Abstracts International, 41,* 3424-A.

Plomin, R. (1983). Child temperament. In B. Lahey & A. Kazdin (Eds.), *Advances in clinical child psychology.* New York: Plenum.

Rahe, R. H. (1974). The pathway between subject's recent life changes and their near-future illness reports: Representative results and methodological issues. In B. S. Dohrenwend & B. P. Dohrenwend (Eds.), *Stressful life events: Their nature and effects.* New York: Wiley.

Rahe, R. H., & Lind, E. (1971). Psychosocial factors and sudden cardiac death: A pilot study. *Journal of Psychosomatic Research, 15,* 19-24.

Rahe, R. H., Mahan, J. L., & Arthur, R. J. (1970). Prediction of near-future health changes from subject's preceding life changes. *Journal of Psychosomatic Research, 14,* 401-406.

Rahe, R. H., & Paasikivi, J. (1971). Psychosocial factors and myocardial infarction—II. An outpatient study in Sweden. *Journal of Psychosomatic Research, 15,* 33-39.

Richter, N. C. (1984). The efficacy of relaxation training with children. *Journal of Abnormal Child Psychology, 12,* 319-344.

Rogosa, D. (1980) A critique of cross-lagged correlation. *Psychological Bulletin, 88,* 245-259.

Rosenman, R. H., Friedman, M., Straus, R., Jenkins, C. D., Zyzanski, S. J., & Messinger, H. B. (1970). Coronary heart disease in the Western Collaborative Group Study: A follow-up experience of four and one-half years. *Journal of Chronic Disabilities, 23,* 173-190.

Ross, C. E., & Mirowsky, J. (1979). A comparison of life-event weighting schemes: Change, undesirability and effect-proportional indices. *Journal of Health and Social Behavior, 20,* 166-177.

Rubin, R. T., Gunderson, E.K.E., & Arthur, R. J. (1971). Life stress and illness patterns in the U.S. Navy—V. Prior life changes and illness onset in a battleship crew. *Journal of Psychosomatic Research, 15,* 89-94.

Rutter, M. (1983). Stress, coping and development: Some issues and some questions. In N. Garmezy & M. Rutter (Eds.), *Stress, coping, and development in children.* New York: McGraw-Hill.

Sandler, I. N., & Block, M. (1979). Life stress and maladaptation of children. *American Journal of Community Psychology, 7,* 425-439.

Sandler, I. N., & Lakey, B. (1982). Locus of control as a stress moderator: The role of control perceptions in social support. *American Journal of Community Psychology, 10,* 65-80.

Sandler, R. N. (1980). Social support resources, stress and maladjustment of poor children. *American Journal of Community Psychology, 8,* 41-52.

Sarason, I. G., Johnson, J. H., & Siegel, J. M. (1978). Assessing the impact of life changes: Development of the Life Experiences Survey. *Journal of Consulting and Clinical Psychology, 46,* 932-946.

Sarason, I. G., Sarason, B. R., & Johnson, J. H. (1985). Stressful life events: Measurement, moderators and adaptation. In S. R. Burchfield (Ed.), *Psychological and physiological interactions in the response to stress.* Washington, DC: Hemisphere.

Schwartz, S., & Johnson, J. H. (1985). *Psychopathology of childhood: A clinical-experimental approach* (2nd ed.). New York: Pergamon.

Segal, J. (1983). Utilization of stress and coping research. In N. Garmezy & M. Rutter (Eds.), *Stress, coping, and development in children.* New York: McGraw-Hill.

Selye, H. (1936). A syndrome produced by diverse nocuous agents. *Nature, 138,* 32.

Selye, H. (1982). History and present status of the stress concept. In L. Goldberger & S. Breznitz (Eds.), *Handbook of stress: Theoretical and Clinical Aspects.* New York: Free Press.

Siegel, J. M., Johnson, J. H., & Sarason, I. G. (1979). Life stress and menstrual discomfort. *Journal of Human Stress, 5,* 41-46.

Siegel, L. J. (1983). Hospitalization and medical care of children. In C. E. Walker & M. C. Roberts (Eds.), *Handbook of clinical child psychology.* New York: John Wiley.

Smith, M. S., Gad, M. T., & O'Grady, L. (1983). Psychosocial functioning, life change, and clinical status in adolescents with cystic fibrosis. *Journal of Adolescent Health Care, 4,* 230-234.

Smith, R. E., Johnson, J. H., & Sarason, I. G. (1978). Life change, the sensation seeking motive, and psychological distress. *Journal of Consulting and Clinical Psychology, 46,* 348-349.

Spivack, G., & Shure, M. B. (1982). The cognition of social adjustment: Interpersonal cognitive problem solving thinking. In B. Lahey & A. Kazdin (Eds.), *Advances in clinical child psychology.* New York: Plenum.

Stein, S. P., & Charles, E. (1971). Emotional factors in juvenile diabetes mellitus: A study of early life experiences of adolescent diabetics. *American Journal of Psychiatry, 128,* 56-60.

Sterling, S., Cowen, E. L., Weissberg, R. P., Lotyczewski, B. S., & Boike, M. (1985). Recent stressful life events and young children's school adjustment. *American Journal of Community Psychology, 13,* 87-99.

Strober, M. (1981). The significance of bulimia in juvenile anorexia nervosa: An exploration of possible etiological factors. *International Journal of Eating Disorders, 1,* 28-43.

Strober, M. (1984). Stressful life events associated with bulimia in anorexia nervosa. *International Journal of Eating Disorders, 3,* 1-13.

Suls, J., & Fletcher, B. (1985). Self-attention, life stress, and illness: A prospective study. *Psychosomatic Medicine, 47,* 469-475.

Swearingen, E. M., & Cohen, L. H. (1985a). Measurement of adolescent's life events: The Junior High Life Experiences Survey. *American Journal of Community Psychology, 13,* 69-85.

Swearingen, E. M., & Cohen, L. H. (1985b). Life events and psychological distress: A prospective study of young adolescents. *Developmental Psychology, 21,* 1045-1054.

Theorell, T., & Rahe, R. H. (1971). Psychosocial factors and myocardial infarction. I: An inpatient study in Sweden. *Journal of Psychosomatic Research, 15,* 25-31.

Thoits, P. A. (1983). Dimensions of life events that influence psychological distress: An evaluation and synthesis of the literature. In H. B. Kaplan (Ed.), *Psychosocial stress: Trends in theory and research.* New York: Academic Press.

Thomas, A., & Chess, S. (1977). *Temperament and development.* New York: Brunner/ Mazel.

Tolor, A., & Murphy, V. M. (1985). Stress and depression in high school students. *Psychological Reports, 57,* 535-541.

Tolor, A., Murphy, V., Wilson, L. T., & Clayton, J. (1983). The High School Readjustment Scale: An attempt to quantify stressful events in young people. *Research Communications in Psychology, Psychiatry and Behavior, 8,* 85-111.

Uhlenhuth, E. H., Shelby, J., Haberman, S. J., Balter, M. D., & Lipman, R. S. (1977). Remembering life events. In J. S. Strauss, H. M. Babigian & M. Roff (Eds.), *The origins and course of psychopathology.* New York: Plenum.

Vaux, A., & Ruggiero, M. (1983). Stressful life change and delinquent behavior. *American Journal of Community Psychology, 11,* 169-183.

Vinokur, A., & Selzer, M. L. (1975). Desirable versus undesirable life events: Their relationship to stress and mental distress. *Journal of Personality and Social Psychology, 32,* 329-337.

Vossel, G., & Froehlich, W. D. (1978). Life stress, job tension, and subjective reports of task performance effectiveness: A causal-correlational analysis. Paper presented at the Conference on Environmental Stress, Life Crisis, and Social Adaptation, Cambridge, England.

Wallerstein, J. (1985). Children of divorce: Preliminary report of a ten-year follow up of older children and adolescents. *Journal of the American Academy of Child Psychiatry, 24,* 545-553.

Wallerstein, J. S. (1983). Children of divorce: Stress and developmental tasks. In M. Garmezy & M. Rutter (Eds.), *Stress, coping and development in children.* New York: McGraw-Hill.

Wallston, K., Wallston, B., & DeVellu, R. (1978). Development of the multidimensional health locus of control scales. *Health Education Monographs, 6,* 160-170.

Watson, D. B. (1983). *The relationship of genital herpes and life stress as moderated by locus of control and social support.* (Doctoral dissertation, University of Southern California). *Dissertation Abstracts International, 43* (A-12), 3857-3858.

Wenet, G. (1979). Life stress and the adolescent sexual offender: A comparative study. Unpublished manuscript, University of Washington.

Wolpe, J. (1958). *Psychotherapy by reciprocal inhibition.* Stanford, CA: University Press.

Wyler, A. R., Masuda, M., & Holmes, T. H. (1971). Magnitude of life events and seriousness of illness. *Psychosomatic Medicine, 33,* 115-122.

Yamamoto, K., & Felsenthal, H. M. (1982). Stressful experiences of children: Professional judgments. *Psychological Reports, 50,* 1087-1093.

Yeaworth, R. C., York, J., Hussey, M. A., Ingle, M. E., & Goodwin, T. (1980). The development of an adolescent life change event scale. *Adolescence, 15,* 91-98.

AUTHOR INDEX

151

SUBJECT INDEX